I Remember

Bob Collins

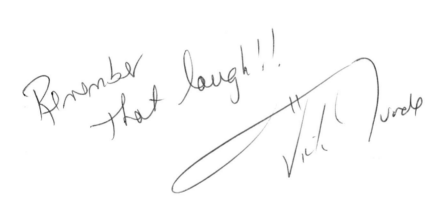

Remember that laugh!!

Vicki Quade

By Vicki Quade

Foreword by Wally Phillips

Dust Jacket Design: Christina Cary
Interior Design: Michelle A. Summers

ISBN: 1-58261-305-2
Library of Congress Catalog Card Number: 00-103333

Bannon Multimedia Group
804 North Neil Street
Champaign, Illinois 61820
www.BMGpub.com

Printed in the United States

Contents

Acknowledgments

When Joe Bannon Jr. called me February 2000 with an offer to write a book about Bob Collins, I accepted the task immediately. I always thought Bob was a tremendous talent, and his death was a great loss to Chicago.

My thanks to my good friend Adrienne Drell, *Chicago Sun-Times* reporter and editor of the book *20th Century Chicago: 100 Years, 100 Voices,* for suggesting my name to Joe.

I am forever grateful to Michelle Summers, managing editor at Bannon Multimedia Group, for her help, insights, suggestions, and cheerful messages. She was a great booster and a great researcher.

I must thank Don Metzger, who opened his address book and helped me track down so many of Bob's Milwaukee friends. I was honored to be invited to the Milwaukee Broadcasters Club's tribute to Bob and introduced as his biographer.

Paul Gallis, one of Bob's closest friends, was also instrumental in opening doors.

Wally Phillips and Roy Leonard were early supporters of the book and freely gave their time and memories. So did Dan Fabian and Lee Rothman, who helped pull together WGN and Milwaukee information.

I'd especially like to thank Bob Bonesteel of the Salvation Army in Chicago, who opened his photo file and allowed me a glimpse of Bob's charity work over the years.

My one regret is that I did not have enough time to interview another 100 people, who I am sure will never forgive me for not getting to them in time. For this, I apologize. No slight was intended!

Many others were contacted including coworkers and family members, who were emotionally unable to provide their own comments but appreciated being asked. I would like to thank all of them for their support.

I have tried to present a balanced view of Bob through interviews with family members, close friends, co-workers, politicians, and fans. I wanted his story to come through their voices. I hope I have succeeded.

And, finally, I must thank my three children, Michael, David, and Catherine, who spent weeks asking me, "Mom, are you on the computer again?" I'm happy they seldom complained about the many frozen dinners they consumed during the course of this project. Now that it's done, I promise to take them to all the movies they missed.

—Vicki Quade

Foreword

Wally Phillips

Wally Phillips is a legendary radio talk show host in Chicago. His retirement from WGN left an opening that was filled by Bob Collins. Phillips is now the host of the Saturday morning program at WAIT-AM.

Somewhere in my swiftly deteriorating memory is the recollection of a phrase that advises: "Only the good die young."

I can't pay tribute to the author by name, nor can I verify whether this is gospel or conjecture.

But I am nourished by its assurance. And the antidote it provides comforts me as I ponder the loss of a friend in the prime and promise of existence.

The premature passing of Bob Collins and the sadness it begets leave us in wonder.

A man of vigor and vitality, compassion and concern, and a joyous contributor enhancing each new day is suddenly no more.

Or is that also conjecture or gospel?

Could it be that his departure is but a chapter in the imponderable mystery we long to comprehend?

An inexplicable that cannot be perceived?

We hunger for resolution. The dilemma endures.

But there are those who view all of this with certainty.

A most reverend predecessor, Mohandas K. Gandhi, said: "There is an indefinable Power that pervades all things. I feel it but I can't see it. It is that power that provides reason for us to hope. To endure."

The Roman orator Cicero made a statement regarding death. He said that day you consider the worst of all days is in reality only your Birthday in Eternity.

Hope is our strength, the guardian of tomorrow.

So thank you, Bob, for being a part of us for a while.

Miss you now. See you anon.

Introduction

The airwaves don't seem the same. Where is that big, infectious laugh? That irreverent look at the world? Where is Bob Collins?

It's hard to imagine that he's not coming back. He was such a regular guy more like your brother or your neighbor. Close friends and colleagues repeat the same description: He was the same on the air as he was off. What you saw is what you got.

The morning-drive host at WGN-AM 720 in Chicago, Collins was one of the key forces behind the station's success. He arrived there in 1974 from Kansas City, from a station he had only worked at for a while. Really, Collins came from Milwaukee, where he had dominated two of its top stations, WOKY and WRIT.

He was hired at WGN to fill the Monday-through-Friday-afternoon and Saturday-night slots, where his irreverent style woke up a sleepy radio giant.

Although WGN was one of the most successful radio operations in the country, it had a reputation for being old and staid. Bruce DuMont of the Museum of Broadcast Communications called it a bastion for baritone announcers whose careers began in the 1930s and '40s: Franklyn MacCormack, John Mallow, and Carl Greyson.

Profound changes were needed to keep its audiences from switching to FM radio. The 32-year-old Collins seemed a perfect fit. With his background in rock 'n' roll and his iconoclastic style, he could attract a new generation of listeners. His audience grew over the next 12 years.

When Wally Phillips, a legend in Chicago radio, decided to retire in 1986 from WGN, management's choice to succeed him seemed impossible. Wally talked about big bands; Bob talked about "Poke Salad Annie." Wally knew the value of a suit and tie. Bob wore mostly T-shirts and jeans. How would Wally's fans accept this loud, smart-alecky guy with a penchant for rock 'n' roll?

If Arbitron ratings are an indication, they liked him just fine.

Lots of people didn't care for his down-home style, but plenty of others tuned in each day to hear what "Uncle Bobby" had to say.

Sure he was different from Wally. He always said he didn't try to be like his predecessor. He didn't have to be. He had his own distinctive style. And he enjoyed rocking the boat. When he couldn't get away from some of the WGN traditions, Bob mocked them, and listeners tuned in every day for more. Where Wally would introduce the agribusiness report as a serious part of WGN programming, Collins had his own approach. He had never spent much time on a farm and often admitted that the business of farming was a mystery to him. He referred to the daily report as "midmorning hogs and frogs." How could you not love that?

He was the only radio figure in Chicago with a double-digit share of the radio audience, unheard of in the highly competitive market. His 10.4 share was almost twice that of listeners of his closest competitors, Felicia Middlebrooks and Ken Herrera at the all-news station WBBM-AM 780.

He was also first in the time slot among listeners ages 25 to 54, a key advertising demographic.

In an age of shock jocks and screamers with megabuck contracts, Bob Collins was a throwback. As successful as he had become, he was still just Bob. He could be blunt, but not rude. He was opinionated, but he didn't cram it down your throat. It was a style that clicked with audiences in one of the toughest radio cities in America.

To appreciate his work, you only have to realize that Bob was on the air four hours a day, five days a week. Not many breaks for music or commercials—Bob read those, too. His replacement, Spike O'Dell, says he wonders now how Bob did it so effortlessly.

It came to an end that Tuesday afternoon, February 8, 2000. Three lives were lost when two planes' ill-fated approaches to Runway 23 at Waukegan Regional Airport resulted in a crash. Collins was killed along with his passenger, Herman Luscher, a retired Navy aviator who flew corporate jets. Also killed was the other pilot, Sharon Hock, a United Airlines flight attendant who friends say was excited about the possibility of flying as a profession.

The Czech-made Zlin 242 was a favorite of Bob's. It was an acrobatic aircraft, perfect for a man who liked to live a little bit on the edge. Collins' love of planes, motorcycles, and fast cars was well known.

Hock's Cessna was considered an industry standard, sturdy and reliable.

The planes collided over downtown Zion, Illinois. Collins must have struggled to steer his severely damaged plane away from buildings and busy Sheridan Road. His plane slammed into the roof of the Midwestern Regional Medical Center in Zion and exploded.

Hock crashed two blocks away in the parking lot of a nursing home and skidded to a stop in the middle of a neighborhood street, about 50 feet from nearby homes.

Given those facts, it's amazing more people weren't hurt or killed.

Collins was born Harold Wallace Lee on February 28, 1942, in Knoxville, Tennessee. His mother was the former Lorraine Ellenburg. His father was Harold Lee.

His early years were rough, family members say. His parents went their separate ways, and his mother remarried when her son was still in grade school. Her new husband, Jack Packett, would become Bob's most important male role model.

He began his radio career at age 13 in Lakeland, Florida, at a local radio station after school, doing odd jobs. By the time he was 14, he had his own afternoon program on WONN. He used the name he grew up with, Buddy Lee. Everyone called him Buddy. He worked his way through school at other small stations throughout Florida, always as a disc jockey.

Around this time, he also broke his leg in a motorcycle accident and limped for a couple of years. While the leg was still in a cast, Buddy begged his stepfather, Jack, to drive him to work.

Wally Phillips

When he wasn't at the radio station, he was at the drums. Buddy Lee played in the high-school band and had visions of his own rock group. When his grades slipped, Jack stepped in and took away Buddy's driving privileges until he got back on track.

He attended the University of Florida and studied journalism, but radio was his first true love. Buddy was married, briefly, for the first time. Her name was Judy Gorman, and she was the widow of Buddy's mentor. It didn't work out, but they stayed friends.

Bob Collins

He returned to his home state to finish his degree at the University of Tennessee but almost immediately landed a radio job. At WKGN in Knoxville, listeners heard him use the name Bob Collins for the first time.

Around this time, Buddy's mother, Lorraine, died of cancer. Jack Packett remarried, and his new wife, Candi, became stepmother to Buddy.

In 1967, calling himself Robert L. Collins, he showed up on Jack Lee's doorstep at WOKY in Milwaukee and said, "I'm looking for a job playing rock 'n' roll and talkin' dirty." Lee hired him instead to do a job that would change his life: a talk show called WOKY TOKY. Collins was a natural for it. (Collins later returned the favor. Jack created the character Fern Quimby Melrose, the Lady of Charm, and she was a favorite with Bob's listeners in Chicago.)

After two years Bob left WOKY for KFI in Los Angeles and a year later began at KCBQ in San Diego. A year after that, Collins returned to Milwaukee to work at WRIT. His former management at WOKY lured him back.

His Milwaukee days were filled with every kind of emotion he could experience. He dated co-workers, hung out at local bars, played Lou Rawls on the jukebox. He married Valerie Voss, a Milwaukee TV personality, but the marriage couldn't withstand their separate career goals. Voss would go on to become CNN's senior meteorologist before retiring recently. After Bob's death, friends got the word to her; she was sailing around the world with her new husband. Bob had that effect on people; they wanted to stay in touch with him.

He had a knack for friendship. He was the kind of guy who would offer an 18-year-old kid a home in his basement. When the kid, hired as a summer fill-in, went on to become president of America Online, Bob still referred to his friend, Bob Pittman, as the "kid who lived in my basement." It was the ultimate one-upsmanship.

He liked to live in the country and took homes away from the hustle and bustle of life. He'd sit out by the lake near his home in Oconomowoc, Wisconsin, with Lee Rothman, enjoying a few drinks and planning the music schedule. He had a casual approach to work but was professional nonetheless.

He had a programming stint at WMYQ in Miami for nine months and was doing some work in Kansas City when Paul Gallis, a well-known record promoter, recommended Collins to the guys at WGN for their afternoon slot. They were looking for someone young who might appeal to a different audience. Gallis had met the young Collins in Milwaukee and liked his style.

In 1974, Bob landed in Chicago, a city he would quickly make his own. You might as well say he was hired on the spot after his audition. WGN knew they had something in this guy.

In 1984, he received the Illinois News Broadcasters Association Award for his on-the-spot news coverage of the Chicago El crash. That same year, *Billboard* Magazine named him Personality of the Year, and in 1987, *Sun-Times* readers chose him as Chicago's Favorite Morning Radio Personality.

He liked to eat and he liked to drink. It wasn't unusual for him to take his friends out to Arlington Raceway to watch the horses run, or to the Bears game. The McCaskey family became close friends. So did Dick Duchossois.

When friends would come to visit him in Chicago, he was a gracious host. Bob Barry once asked him what it was like to be a celebrity. Collins was quick to answer that cab drivers wouldn't even know who he was. He was a radio guy, not a face on television. Still, he had that voice, that unmistakable voice. When he opened his mouth to speak, the fans came around for autographs.

While radio was his home, Bob did some work on WGN television, focusing a program on the Concorde Airliner, and a piece on the history of Wrigley Field, home of the Chicago Cubs. His attempts at learning to play baseball with the Cubs made for great comedy. He also tried his hand at writing. He accepted the *Daily Herald*'s offer to write a weekly column and had already started to grow as a writer.

Collins spent a considerable amount of time raising funds for various causes, but his two favorites were the Salvation Army and the WGN Neediest Kids Fund. Twice he was named Man of the Year by the local chapter of the Salvation Army. For years, he was on hand to light to Salvation Army's Christmas tree in front of the John Hancock building.

He enjoyed politicians and was unabashadly Republican. He socialized with Illinois governors Jim Thompson, Jim Edgar, and George Ryan, even emceeing Edgar's inauguration bash.

Collins' hobbies included flying, motorcycles and collecting cars. He took his first flying lesson in a Cessna 152 on December 31, 1977. He owned his first motorcycle at age 12. Jim Dowdle of the Tribune Company said Bob had so many cars, he qualified as a dealer.

Away from the microphone, Bob Collins preferred a private life. He had been hanging around the Experimental Aircraft Association, in Oshkosh, Wisconsin, and had met Jim Barton, one of the pilots there. Jim had a daughter, Christine, with a pretty face and long, blond hair. Bob was smitten.

After they were married, he called her "Old Agnes" on the air. Eventually, listeners got to know her name. Bob couldn't keep that secret for long.

Friends called them soul mates. The two enjoyed traveling and had his and her Harleys. They joined a group of bikers who made regular Sunday morning stops at the Highland House in Highland Park. The eggs were good, the conversation was better.

And then there was his dog Booger, Bob's other love. Chicagoans will forever be in Chris Collins' debt for suggesting the name to her husband. It gave Bob license to use the word "booger" on the air whenever he wanted.

Collins had recently signed a five-year, multimillion-dollar contract with WGN, negotiated by Chicago lawyer Todd Musburger. It was the first time he had used a professional agent to negotiate his contract.

Chicago has lost many prominent figures in recent years, including Harry Caray, Jack Brickhouse, Walter Payton, Mike Royko, and Gene Siskel. Wally Phillips calls them "an endless stream of good guys." Bob now joins that group.

—Vicki Quade

Chapter 1

Formative Years

Roy Stanek

Bob and Christine Collins

For Those Who Touched His Life

Christine Collins

Christine Collins, Bob's wife, was known as "Old Agnes" to his listeners. Christine's comments were made at the Milwaukee Broadcasters Association tribute to Bob Collins.

Just about everybody had some kind of a touch with Bob somewhere along the line. He meant a lot to me, but you are the people who helped touch his life all the way along.

The Early Life of Buddy Lee and the Influences That Made Him Bob Collins

Jack Packett

Jack Packett is Bob Collins' stepfather. He lives in Lakeland, Florida, and is a retired buyer for the Publix supermarket chain.

I was married to Buddy's mother, Lorraine. Her maiden name was Ellenburg. We met in Knoxville. I had just gotten out of college and got a job with Swift & Co., and then I was transferred to Lakeland, Florida.

She moved with me to Lakeland and we were married. This was around 1950. Buddy must have been about eight or 10 years old. He was still in grade school. He was an altar boy at St. Joseph's church in Lakeland. A good student.

We used to go to the beach all the time. And ride dirt bikes in what they call the pits; it's where phosphate was mined. He liked to play the drums. He liked to fish, but didn't want to catch them. He didn't believe in hurting anything.

He was always well taken care of, never had any problems. He was a good student, until the band got to be pretty important to him. He let his grades slip and we had a little problem. He eventually graduated from high school with good grades. You know how? He had an automobile, well, he had several, and I would take them away from him. I'd say, "You can't drive." And he would offer me the keys and I'd say, "No, I don't want the keys; you just can't drive." That was the only thing I could do to get his grades up. It worked.

He went to the University of Florida for a while. But he liked to water ski. And eventually he got a job announcing the shows at Cypress Gardens and went on a couple of big tours with them.

He came back to Lakeland and went to Southern College for a while, then wanted to go to the University of Tennessee. He got off the train, and got a job at the radio station. I don't think he ever entered the University of Tennessee, to tell you the truth. I'm not sure he went to a single class. After that he went all over the country on the radio.

He had his name legally changed. Bob Collins had a better ring than Harold Wallace Lee or Buddy Lee. It was something he wanted to do to make it easier for people to recognize his name.

He was from the Virginia Lees, not Irish. He was anything he wanted to be. If he wanted to be Irish one day, he was Irish. If he wanted to be Greek one day, he was Greek.

I loved him deeply, and I think he loved me deeply. I never had a moment's problem with him. I always enjoyed being with him, and he always enjoyed our company. We traveled a bit, all over the country. He loved the West Coast up to the Northwest and Canada. He loved Arizona. Florida just got too hot for him; he didn't like the humidity. But I love it.

He got so much enjoyment out of his work. It was his work that kept him on the straight and narrow, that gave him a purpose in life. He loved his work; he loved what he did. Couldn't stay away from it too long. Didn't make any difference where he was.

He liked working in San Diego. He liked Milwaukee and had many good friends there. The only place he didn't like was Los Angeles, too much puff and pastry for him.

I miss his voice, his calling on the phone. He'd call up and say, "Don't say cuss words 'cause we're going to be on the air." And I'd say, "How many cuss words have you ever heard me say?" and he'd say, "I don't know, just be careful!"

He'd run personal things by me. He'd talk about retiring, whether he should take another five years. I wanted him to take the five years. He could quit at anytime, but I thought he should do another five years and take the contract. We talked about all the ordinary things in your life that you're not sure you know what you want to do.

I'm not saying he took my advice, but I was always more than happy to give it.

Bob's Stepmom Remembers a Loving Son

Candi Packett

Candi Packett is Bob's stepmother. She lives in Lakeland, Florida, and works selling real estate for Century 21.

We always call him Buddy, even though I know everybody else calls him Bob. He was Buddy to us. I don't know why he changed his name to Bob Collins. Just picked it out one day and started using it. God knows where he got it from. I guess he thought it was a better name.

People think he's Irish, but I don't think he is. I'm not sure what the name Lee is.

His mother passed away around 1965 from cancer, and I married his stepfather, Jack. We've been married 35 years. When I first met Buddy, he was in his early 20s. He had hair down to his waist and was really skinny.

From the time he was 14, he was into radio. He started over here in Lakeland at a radio station, just a runner. He always loved it and it became his life.

I got a letter from Jack's niece, Linda Essary, talking about Buddy. She was younger than he. He would bring her records and things like that from the radio station because he thought she'd like them. He was very thoughtful that way, even when he was younger.

I have four children, and he was real close with my younger two, especially the youngest one, Kim. That was his baby sister as far as he was concerned. Buddy has a younger half-sister, Janet, from his father's side. I know Kim met her with Buddy about 20 years ago. I talked with her at the funeral, and she told me about Buddy's early years. His birth father was evidently an alcoholic. Things weren't very easy for Buddy.

He was a bookworm when he was younger. He always had a book in his hand. Even when he would sit for a meal, he read books. Always reading, all the time. He was very private, but he also was very good to stay in touch. As he got older, we heard from him three or four times a week. He'd call us and make sure everything was okay. Very thoughtful. I always said he was more thoughtful than my own children were!

Buddy was the kind of man who kept friends. He was married for a short time while he lived in Florida. In fact, I got a nice letter from Judy, his first wife. I think her name was Judy Gorman when they married. It was something that should have never been. Her husband had passed away and he was Buddy's mentor. I think Buddy felt he should take care of her, but it didn't work out. But they remained friends.

Later he married Valerie Voss. She was nice. She became a weatherperson. I never really asked what went wrong there, but I always thought they still loved each other after the divorce. He had his career and she wanted hers, and it was one of those things.

We were happy when he met Christine. I don't think Buddy changed because of Christine, but he was certainly happy. In fact, I think he always stayed the same, no matter what happened to him. That was the way it was with him.

He was one of those that stayed in touch with everybody. Dan Fabian, his friend from Chicago, said, "I always thought I was his best friend," but when he talked with everybody at the funeral, they all felt the same way.

Buddy even kept in touch with fellows he went to school with. Yet he was a private person. When we went to the Marconi Awards, he would go, but he'd leave quietly. As public as he was, he wanted to stay private. He was just that way.

He never had children; didn't want them. He liked other people's children and he was good with them, but he never wanted any for himself. I think he saw so many of his friends with breakups in their marriages and how that affects kids, he didn't want that for himself. Instead, he had dogs, loved dogs, always had a dog. Passionately loved dogs. Those were his children.

And he loved cars, and motorcycles. He had motorcycles when he was a teenager. He even had an accident as a teenager, broke his leg. His stepfather, Jack, had to drive him to work everyday at the radio station.

He limped for two years.

He would go fishing but he wouldn't catch fish because he didn't like killing animals, but he wasn't a vegetarian or anything like that. He didn't go that far.

I'm going to miss his calls. His hearty laugh and all. He was always concerned about what we were doing, what the kids were up to. I'll miss that. He'd always call early in the morning, which was fine with me because I'm an early riser. And we'd get together a couple of times a year.

In fact, he was here just a week before the accident. He flew down. He stopped off here to visit and spend the night, but he was really on his way to Naples, Florida. He had a friend down there who was dying. A few weeks before he had gone down to see this fellow. They didn't expect him to live. He wanted a corned beef sandwich, so Buddy went out and got him one. He said, "If he's going to die, he might as well go out happy."

Evidently he turned around and now he's doing better! Funny how that stuff happens.

Buddy didn't like crowds. When we went out to dinner, he liked it quiet. He was around crowds all the time, so he didn't like them when he was on his own time. We'd go down to the club, where it's private. He loved to eat collard greens, black-eyed peas, and cornbread. That was one of his favorite meals.

How Buddy Lee Became Bob Collins

Tom Kennington

Tom Kennington is director of Film and Television Development, at the Disney-MGM Studios in Florida.

I first met Bob, or Buddy (I knew him as Buddy Lee), when my family moved to Lakeland, Florida, in the fall of 1956. We lived on one corner of South Crystal Lake Drive and Buddy and his fam-

Bob Collins and Tom Kennington on remote from Walt Disney World

ily lived directly across the street on the other corner. I was just entering the 10th grade and Buddy was one year younger than I was, but I soon learned that we had two things very much in common: our love for music (particularly rock 'n' roll) and our burning desire to get into radio and become disc jockeys.

In those early days of our friendship in '56 and '57, we used to "play" radio. We would make microphones out of wood blocks and, using our small record players as turntables, we would take turns reading the news out of the paper. We honed our deejay skills preparing for the day when we could do it for real.

We both got our first jobs in radio while still in high school. I started at one of the local Lakeland stations, WLAK, and Buddy started at the other, WONN. Following graduation I headed off to the University of Florida and worked my way through school at WDVH. Buddy also followed his dream into radio.

While I was at WDVH, I received an air check from Buddy while he was at WKGN in Knoxville, Tennessee, and heard him use the name Bob Collins for the first time. I never called him Buddy again.

Even though we stayed in touch over the years, we never worked in the same town until the mid-'70s, when I was program director at WFUN in Miami and Bob was programming WMYQ-FM. A couple of years before Bob got to WMYQ, it had become one of the first, if not *the* first, FM station to play rock 'n' roll, or "Top 40" as it was called then.

When Bob arrived, we were in a full-tilt ratings race. I was fighting a losing battle to keep an AM station in music competition with an FM. Bob was single then, and his apartment became kind of a hangout and haven for people in the radio and record business.

I remember one night Mark Lindsay, lead singer with Paul Revere and the Raiders, was in town and we had dinner together and decided to stop by and see Bob. While there, for some reason, Mark decided to go outside and look around. Shortly thereafter, he came back with this strange look on his face. He said that he had bumped into a very pretty young lady and had said, "Hi, I'm Mark Lindsay," and she said, "Sure you are," and just kept walking. Bob and I thought this was very funny!

At the time Bob was hired at WGN, I had become the national program director for the Rounsaville chain of radio stations and called to congratulate him. I so distinctly remember him saying how nervous he was because both of us were used to how things worked in "Top 40," where the disc jockey had to do everything.

Bob was just astonished that he had a producer, newspeople, people to answer the phones, and even an announcer who would come in once an hour and say, "WGN, Chicago."

Our friendship continued to grow, and when I joined the marketing department of Walt Disney World, I would always look forward to the times he would come down and originate his show from one of our parks during some special event. Bob had married his lovely and wonderful wife Chris by then, and it was such a pleasure to get to know her. Chris was a real Disney fan and would spend her time visiting the many Disney shops (much to the delight of all of our stockholders) while Bob was on the air.

On most of his visits I would go on the show and talk about what was new at Walt Disney World, and Bob would love to introduce me by saying, "Tom remembers me when I was skinny, and I remember him when he had hair!!"

On his visits during the past few years we would spend time talking about our plans for retirement. This was especially the topic on his last visit a few months before his death. He was so looking forward to the time he and Chris would have to do just the things they both loved to do.

Then there was that night when I was channel-surfing and ran across one of the news channels that reported a midair collision that had claimed the life of a prominent Chicago radio personality. My first thought was, *no,* it couldn't be. Then it was reported, "WGN's Bob Collins was killed today." I felt like I had been hit in the stomach by a big fist.

At that moment I flashed back to those innocent days in 1956, "playing radio" and looking forward to the future with my friend and neighbor from across the street.

I know that Chicago will greatly miss this warm, jovial friend who woke them up each morning, but there are a lot of us in Florida who also feel the loss. God bless you, Chris, and remember that we are always here!

• • • • • • •

Chapter 2

Milwaukee Years

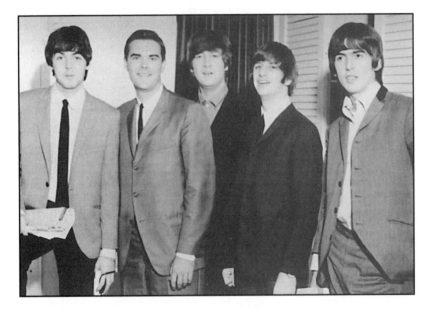

(Left to right) Paul McCartney, Bob Barry, John Lennon, Ringo Starr and George Harrison

He Treated Us All as Equals

Bob Barry

Bob Barry worked with Bob Collins at WOKY.

I was always Beatle Bob to him on the air. I had interviewed the Beatles in '64, and Bob always remembered that. He'd kid me about that.

We used to double-date a lot. We'd go into the same watering holes. One of them was Frankie's on Brady Street in Milwaukee. It was one of his favorite places because the jukebox had all the Lou

Rawls stuff on there. Some of them were obscure cuts that were sort of bluesy, heartache stuff. He was going through a rough time. He was dating a couple of young ladies, and they were going through the tough early stages of dating.

I was dating an airline stewardess who was a real doll. Bob loved to tell her stories about me that were kind of half-truths. He told her all this stuff because he wanted to date her, but she ended up giving us both the heave-ho.

That down-home thing of Bob's caught on here in Milwaukee in the '60s, but not as big as it did in Chicago. Milwaukee was shocked by some of the things he did.

Stuff like playing Tony Joe White's "Poke Salad Annie;" he would really milk that thing on the air. Repeating the lyrics really slowly. "Gator got your granny." That kind of stuff. He'd do it in that southern drawl. Milwaukee at the time was very conservative. They weren't quite ready for that. The young people liked it, though.

Bobby was a rebel when I first met him. He came in and I said, "What the heck." He'd go on the air and say, "Mother Puckett's son, Gary." That just wasn't done. He was the first guy to use the word "jockstrap" on the air.

There were a lot of terms he used that we weren't used to. He opened the doors for a lot of us that way. We kept right on going after that.

He'd come to work in matching turtlenecks and Levis. If you saw him in a tie, you'd be shocked. It was only when he was told he must wear a tie that he'd wear one.

One time he was at the WOKY Christmas party. He got up on stage toward the end of the evening and brought three other people up there. He said, "This is a great party, we really had a good time. Thanks a lot for the bonus. I want you all to know the four of us are going to WRIT starting Monday."

And then they walked out. He wasn't kidding. He was really leaving the station to go to WRIT. And that's how he announced it. We were all laughing, but the bosses weren't. Their faces dropped.

He loved that shock kind of stuff, not only on the air, but off the air, too.

He never wanted the limelight. We'd do personal appearances and he'd build me up while he stood in the background. He wasn't timid, but he just liked to see other people be successful. He always treated me like we were equals, even after he got the job in Chicago and started making millions.

We had a mutual friend, Jim Brown, who died in March of 1999. When Jim came to Chicago, Bob would take us out to the track at Arlington or out to dinner.

Jim Brown had been one of the program directors at WOKY, but later on he was kind of down on his luck. He probably had a couple thousand dollars to his name. But Bob treated him like he was an equal. Bob was that kind of guy. It didn't matter how much money you had.

Jim's death really affected Bob. And Bob had another friend, Scott Anderson, who died in a plane crash. Jim and this Scott Anderson died within a week of each other. That really affected Bob.

We did lots of record hops together. CYO dances on Friday night. We would book three in one night. We would get most of those appearances. Four of us: Jack Lee, Jim Brown, Bob Collins, and myself would do these on Friday nights. Then we'd meet afterward, play cards. Bob loved to gamble.

Sometimes down in the basement, we'd have a couple thousand dollars on the table down there. There were a lot of times they were playing at my house I'd just go upstairs and go to bed. It got to be too rich for my blood. It wasn't that Bob was making a lot of money then; it's that he loved to gamble.

When he met Chris, his whole life changed. He changed, his program changed, he became a very mature guy at that time and very successful.

The last time we were supposed to go to Arlington racetrack with Bob, it was quite an occasion. It started to rain. Pouring rain. So instead of going to Arlington, Bob took us all to Ditka's. Jim Brown did not have a jacket, so Collins asked if we could get a room in the back so Jim didn't have to wear a jacket. We were all by ourselves in the back. We were watching the races.

That was the day Pat Day won all but one race. That's the record that still stands today.

That's the day Bob introduced me to Sambucca. Oh, man. I couldn't believe it.

I thought those were raisins in the bottle instead of coffee beans, so I bit into one. Bob had a good time razzing me about that: "Don't you ever drink?"

The Lady of Charm Gives Bob His Big Break

Jack Lee

Jack Lee worked with Bob Collins in Milwaukee, and created the character of Fern Quimby Melrose, the Lady of Charm, which was featured on Bob's show at WGN. He is retired from the Heritage Media Corporation in Milwaukee.

I hired Bob at WOKY in Milwaukee. I didn't get a lot of background on him, mostly because of the situation of hiring him. I was in a real bind to hire someone. He didn't send a résumé or anything; he just showed up at my door one day, kind of lurking in the doorway.

He said he had come north, I believe, to the Chicago area. He worked for a suburban station. I don't remember the call letters, but the job lasted about a week or 10 days. It was one of these situations where the station got sold or changed format or something like that. He described it as a black and tan station.

Bob was influenced a lot by black disk jockeys. They say Bill Clinton is our first black president; well, Bob Collins was WGN's first black morning personality, truth be known. He had a lot of soul.

Somebody once said they thought Bob worked at a rhythm-and-blues station in Milwaukee. Leonard Chess of Chess Records in Chicago owned an AM station in Milwaukee, and it was being sold at about that time. I think Bob hit that window of inopportunity. He came for that job, and when he got to Milwaukee, the station went away.

(Left to Right) Bob Barry, Tom Petersen, Jack Lee, Don Metzger, Chris Collins, Spike O'Dell; Sitting: Paul Gallis

At that time, disc jockeys were kind of itinerant. It was not unusual at all to do six months here, four months there. Going around the country like gypsies. He ended up in Milwaukee. If I remember correctly, he came to town on a motorcycle.

So he came to see me at WOKY. This was in 1967, I believe. I was not in a position of regular authority at the radio station. I was an air personality at WOKY, which was a Top 40 station. We had a talk show at night to satisfy the public-affairs requirements of the FCC. Two hours, 10 to midnight, called WOKY TOKY. It was highly rated for its time. It had guests usually, and they were controversial. Kind of an early Dr. Laura/Rush Limbaugh kind of show.

The program director of the station hadn't taken a vacation in years. He took a three-week vacation, left town. I was the assistant program director, and I was left in charge.

The host of WOKY TOKY was a highly volatile personality and got into an argument with the owner of the station, on the hotline one night. That led to the owner saying that person would never come into the building again. She told me I'd be doing my show from 9 until noon, I'd be program director, and I'd have to do this WOKY TOKY until I hired someone to replace this guy.

About four days into this sleep-deprived state, I'm sitting in my office when Bob came in. He was about 25, rail thin, like six-foot-two, 140 pounds. And he leaned against the doorway and said, "I'm looking for a job playing rock 'n' roll and talkin' dirty."

I said, "Normally, we have jobs like that here, but the only thing I have right now is a talk show."

And he said, "I've never done it. I don't even read the news. I don't want anything to do with it."

I said, "Sit down, let's get acquainted." We discovered that we were both from Tennessee. I professionally was Jack Lee; his real name was Harold Lee.

He was from Knoxville, Tennessee; my wife was from Knox-ville. So we put our feet up and did good-ole-boy talk.

I was desperate for someone for this night show. I discovered he was a pretty insightful, interesting guy. I said, "Would you be willing to audition for this show?"

He said, "I don't have a tape. I've never done a talk show; it's just not my thing."

I said, "Well, let's go into the studio. We usually have guests; I'll make up a name. I'll be a character. We don't want to be silly about this." So I created this character of a religious leader who was in town, thinking this would be a real test for Bob. And about four minutes into this interview, it was obvious he was brilliant. He was serious; he was respectful at the same time. It was fascinating.

I asked him if he would go on the air that night. He said, "If you'll make me the deal that the first time playing rock 'n' roll and talkin' dirty opens up, I get to get off that talk show and get on the air with the rest of the disc jockeys, I'll do it."

He did about six months, the best host we ever had. A whole different direction for the show.

Sure enough, when an air-personality job opened up, he walked into my office and said, "Remember the promise we had. I want to get on the air and do what I do best. I'm not comfortable doing the other thing."

In a long nutshell, that's how he came to get the experience doing a talk show. I think that did a great deal in giving him the confidence to do what he eventually did at WGN. He always told me that. As fate would have it, having that show in his background really helped.

Soon after Bob started at WOKY, he had a motorcycle and a series of Volvos.

Bob was into exotic machinery even then. He always loved his toys. He was the first person I ever saw with a phone in his car. This was 1967. There were no cellular phones then. A car phone was almost like a phone booth. You'd get into the car with him and you'd barely have room to sit. There was this huge device bolted to the floor.

The first time I got into his car, I made more money than he did, and I didn't make very much money. About every four months, he would show up with a brand-new Volvo. He'd spend a day in the garage having the telephone installed.

Volvos didn't change styles for years, but every four months or so he'd show up with a new one, in a different color. You'd be riding around with him and you'd see something like a Jaguar and say, "Oh man, look at that!" And he'd say, "I didn't like mine. I kept it for about two weeks." I'd say, "You had a Jaguar?" "Yeah," Bob said, "it stopped at a stoplight and I called them to pick it up. Didn't like it."

The same was true for what we called hi-fi equipment. I'd go to his apartment and say, "Didn't you have like a Sansui thing?" And he'd say, "Yeah, I gave that to Jim Brown." About four times a year, he would completely redo all the audio equipment in his apartment. He'd get bored with it, see something that was bright, shiny, and new, and that's what he wanted.

I don't think he had any idea of money management. Luckily in later years he had plenty to work with. I don't know how he was able to do it. He was a very responsible individual. Unlike a lot of air personalities, he always showed up to work on time. He was never in money trouble, like so many of those guys.

He was single. He obviously didn't have a tremendous amount of money resources, but what he had, he spent on toys. He never spent a lot of money on clothes; he liked to play.

I was married at the time with three kids and a cocker spaniel. I was never a big drinker or gambler. Bob was an eligible young single guy. He really enjoyed a good time.

Well, I had created this character at WOKY, I called her the Lady of Charm. I started that in Milwaukee when I was doing middays. It was kind of a frumpy Martha Stewart. She'd give advice to the lovelorn. There was a whole plot developed around her. She lived at Ma Groggin's boarding house, a single girls' retreat on the south side of Milwaukee. She had these friends we developed. She had feuds with Trixie Burlingame. It was like a soap opera. She got involved in everything from running for president to writing a book to going on the road with a polka band.

Bob loved that character and was always so generous with his praise of others and their talents. Well, when Bob got to WGN, he wanted to do something with the Lady of Charm. He thought that was a great bit. He thought it was better than I did.

He was nervous about it because he had never really worked with anyone else. He had always done a single-person act. At the same time, he never required any script, rehearsal, no talking ahead of time. I never knew when I was going to do it. I'd get a call at 5:20 a.m., waking me up. His producer would say, "Bob wants you on the air in three minutes." That's the way he liked to do it, and, frankly, I enjoyed it that way, too.

He wanted to be surprised and react naturally to it. He was the most marvelous straight man. You can imagine some of the material wasn't the best; you came up with it in three minutes! He always made it acceptable and sometimes turned mediocre material into something very good.

Once I was on vacation and Bob wanted to do something, say, on a Friday afternoon. I'd stop at a phone booth and call the hotline at WGN. You'd hear trucks going by. I'd be standing at the phone booth doing the Lady of Charm character. I'd be making up some story of why I was in the middle of Kentucky. I'd be abandoned by Sam Vishniak's polka band. I'd been on a tour with them and they'd left me at a truck stop. Stuff like that.

They played the Lady of Charm thing as part of the two-hour tribute to Bob at WGN. I learned later, after Bob's death, that he enjoyed using the Lady of Charm as a kind of pick-me-up. He enjoyed it so much. If he had a slow day or needed a good laugh, he'd think of that.

We started doing the Lady of Charm on WGN around 1981. At that time, I'd been off the air for a number of years. I was in general management. Bob lobbied regularly for the management of WGN to hire me because he wanted to work with me. He wanted them to create some kind of shift for me so I could sit with him for a couple of hours, and then do a show in the afternoon. Maybe do some early evening stuff.

At that point, I had stock options at my job. It was not a good career move for me.

I was intrigued, because it's a great station. The high point of my career was the opportunity to work with Bob Collins. I've never had that professional bond with anyone else.

Here's another side of Bob that people often saw.

I came to a meeting of the Milwaukee broadcasters. I had to babysit my nine-year-old granddaughter, who was with me. She was bored to tears.

Now, she has a little bit of a gambling weakness. She loves those machines with a claw that goes down to grab a doll. If she sees one of those machines, she'll take all of her allowance with her and feed the machine until she's out of money. She's never gotten anything.

So we get to the meeting and she's pulling on my arm. There's a machine in the corner. I told her, "You know, it always gets your money. You never win anything."

But I gave her two quarters. I'm talking to someone for about 10 minutes and I start looking around for her. I look over and sparks are practically coming out of the machine. Collins is standing there with about 20 dollars in quarters. She still doesn't have anything, but she's having a blast.

He was a very generous man.

An Old Flame Remembers Bob

Kay Simon

Kay Simon worked with Bob at WOKY and dated him for several years. She's a marketing director in San Francisco.

I was part of WOKY when that station went from nothing to the biggest thing in Milwaukee. The team we had was great: Bob Barry, Jack Lee, Bob Collins. Think about it, that was 32 years ago, and we all remember it like it was yesterday. Bob was the glue that kept us all together.

I miss Bob so much, my heart breaks. He was my first love. I was 20 and he was 26, and we were engaged for a short time. We were just too young. As years passed, we developed this wonderful friendship. I became friends with Valerie Voss, who married him sometime later.

When he met Christine, she was his soul mate. She made him the loving, devoted man he is. Years later, Bob and I had this long talk about how he carried guilt about the way he broke my heart. I told him, "Bob, we were so young. It wasn't right."

He and Christine and I became good friends. Whenever the two of them came to San Francisco, they always visited. He loved his job, and it wasn't a job to him. I'd ask him how it was going, and he'd say, "Oh, you know." He never talked about all the dignitaries he was meeting or how popular he was. We talked on our level.

He called me a year ago to tell me that Jim Brown was dead. Jim Brown and I had dated for seven years, so Bob knew how diffi-

Kay Simon (above) was a part of the formidable WOKY team with Bob Barry, Jack Lee and Bob Collins.

cult this would be for me. The truth was, it was so difficult for him to call me. He was having a hard time dealing with the death of close friends.

My sister called me to make sure I had heard Bob Collins was dead. When I got home that night, Bob Barry had called. I hadn't heard from Bob Barry in 30 years, but it was that glue that was keeping us together. It was Bob's glue.

One story I do remember is that when WOKY was not very hot, George Wilson came in. George put together an incredible team and we became number one. None of us was used to this fame. We'd go to dinner at Frenchy's. We'd go into the parking lot and check the car radios to see where their dials were. We'd celebrate. "Here's another WOKY!" It was the very best time.

There was a place across the street from WOKY called the Annex. Sometimes the guys would be at the Annex. If George had a long-distance call from the higher-ups, I'd have to page him at the Annex. That was our little hangout. It was the best part of my life, being there.

We all know how much Christine played a part in Bob's life. We were grateful to her for sharing him with us. I can remember sitting with the two of them, and Bob would be telling stories, then he'd tease Christine with such love. She allowed him to shine.

From Down Home to Talking Dirty

Don Metzger

Don Metzger owns and operates DM Productions in Mequon, Wisconsin.

I first met Bob Collins about 150 pounds ago (his, not mine) when he was hired at WOKY radio to host the night talk show WOKY TOKY (Walkie Talkie). I remember he didn't want to do the talk show. He said, "No, that's not for me." But he was convinced to give it a try.

I had been a rock 'n' roll deejay at WRIT in Milwaukee in the late 1950s and then opened my own ad agency in 1960. Our agency represented WOKY, and I worked with Bob on station promotions.

We would schedule big events at the county stadium in which we'd bring in all the Top 40 stars, like Gary Lewis and the Playboys, the Four Lads, the Lettermen. Just about anyone who had a record in the Top 40 would come into town. Bob really enjoyed those because he enjoyed music. He had a great mind for music.

I enjoyed his quick wit and especially took to his "down home" twang and infectious laugh.

Don Metzger

In late '72 or early '73, he went to work for my alma mater, WRIT. I did commercial recordings there, so I saw him quite often. We'd sometimes go out after work for a beverage or two.

By this time, his style on the air had changed. Gone was the "down-home" guy from WOKY, replaced by Bob's own version of a feisty "Peck's Bad Boy."

Bob would describe himself as a rock 'n' roll jock who liked to talk dirty. When he went to WGN in 1974, I wondered how he'd fit the staid WGN format. I figured either one of them—WGN or Bob—had to change. The winner was WGN—they changed, Bob stayed the same.

I not only was a longtime friend of Bob but a fan as well. I visited him in Chicago and watched him do his morning show. We'd do breakfast at Lou Mitchell's restaurant, which at the time was run by Nick Noble, a former '50s singer and recording star. I could never pick up the tab there. Nick picked up the tab most of the time. But so did Bob. He was a very generous friend.

Bob never forgot his roots and often talked about the Milwaukee Broadcasters Club, of which he became a member. I'm a co-founder of the club, along with Lee Rothman, who also worked with Bob at WRIT.

Lee and I would often act as "end-men" at countless Variety Club roasts. Once, Bob was asked to attend a roast in honor of his former boss at WRIT, Bernie Strachota. But Bob was uncomfortable with the standard roast format, which called for some good-natured ribbing. Bob didn't want to say anything that might offend Bernie, even though that kind of humor was what roasts were all about.

Bob was a magnificent talent. He was the same guy off the air as he was on the air. That's what made him so successful. I'll miss him as a talent and a friend.

An Early Pioneer of Talk Radio

Tony Karr

Tony Karr is retired and lives in Port Washington, Wisconsin.

Bob Collins followed me on the air at WOKY. I was on from 6 to 10, and he was on from 10 to midnight when he started on WOKY TOKY.

We were all young then. As a matter of fact, he is two years younger than I, and I was amazed at that. He seemed much older. I was usually out the door at 10 p.m. to go to the record hops. Bob was doing a talk show and trying to maintain some dignity on the air, which none of us really had.

The interesting point is that in the middle '60s, talk radio barely existed. I came from WOWO in Fort Wayne, Indiana, a Westinghouse 50,000-watt station, very powerful, especially in a town like Fort Wayne. We covered the entire Midwest. At night, the station got into Florida and Louisiana. This was around 1964, and we had on that station a program that was really a magazine show on radio. It was very folksy, a lot of short segments of unusual things. Very difficult to do that kind of show.

The show Bob did, WOKY TOKY, was a different kind of talk radio. You threw out a subject and whoever wanted to call in and talk about it did. But you had to have a breadth of knowledge, because you had to know something about what people were saying on the air. Bob had an intelligence. If you had surveyed rock-'n'-roll disc jockeys at that time, I believe we would have been below the scale of IQ.

It's what he needed to do what he did later on, to have that background. We all wanted to be the disc jockeys out with the kids. How fortunate for Bob's later career that he had that background.

Before Booger, There Was Dammit

Sue Riordan

Sue Riordan is retired and living in Milwaukee.

I was in public relations for Marquette University in Milwaukee, and I booked guests on Bob's talk show on WOKY. We became fast friends. There was a gang of us at WOKY who palled around together.

It's funny. I knew Bob 30 years ago, but when I was listening to the tributes on WGN after his death, I realized that Bob hadn't changed at all. He was still the same caring individual. He really became involved in people's lives. I don't really know why. He came from some interesting family background.

He was so extroverted on the air; so much energy and life poured through the microphone. But off the microphone he was very quiet and introspective. Almost contemplative. Extremely intellectual. He was a voracious reader. He could size up an argument and present both sides in a way that never irritated anybody.

I think it was his generosity and compassion I'll always remember.

You know, he loved dogs. He had a whippet back then. Once after he got that dog, he left it at home when he went to work. The whippet thrashed its tail so much, it must have nicked it, because when Bob got home that day, his whole apartment was filled with blood. After that he took the dog wherever he went.

That dog was named Dammit. "Come here, Dammit," he'd shout. He had the best names for his dogs. People talk about his dog, Booger, but I didn't know that dog. I knew Dammit.

He talked about that dog on the radio, but he couldn't say his name on the radio. That doesn't mean he didn't get away with saying other things. He talked dirty on the radio, but in a funny way. He'd say whatever he could get away with. Always pushing to see what he could do.

We had another guy, Jim Brown, on the radio, and Bob and Jim were good friends. When they got together, the devil would get into the two of them.

You Don't Forget That Kind of Loyalty

Ralph Barnes

Ralph Barnes lives in Manitowish Waters, Wisconsin. He managed radio stations in Milwaukee, Des Moines, and Richmond for several years.

I worked with Bob for about three years. He started at WOKY when I was just a salesman there.

He left WOKY rather abruptly with the program director for a new job in California, then he came back to WRIT, our competitor.

He was a flamboyant egghead. He was a very, very soft touch. A very generous man. Anybody who needed some money, he readily helped that person out, if he knew them! Because of his generosity and good heart, I'm sure he lost money over the years. But he never complained.

I traveled to Washington, D. C., and Los Angeles with him. He was interested in people, more than anything else. We went our separate ways in Washington. He had friends there and I had business. He wasn't one to go sightseeing and look at the buildings. He was happier just sitting and talking, getting to know you.

He had a keen sense of humor, which was, at times, caustic. I could give you an example, but I won't.

The thing I appreciate most is that he never forgot his friends. When the broadcasters in Milwaukee gave me a farewell party, Bob showed up. When they saluted Bob Barry, well, Bob Collins came and congratulated Bob with the rest of us. They had a party for Bernie Strachota's retirement and Bob made it up to Milwaukee for that.

You don't forget that kind of loyalty.

Cherry Pies and Red Faces

Skip Taylor

Skip Taylor was a deejay at WOKY from 1969 to 1976. He is currently owner and operator of RAM Productions in Wausau, Wisconsin.

One thought that lingers in my mind is that Bob was fully aware of the hazards of flying. In 1974, I was working as the night-time deejay at WOKY in Milwaukee. Bob was my boss, and I was the rookie. I wanted to spend as much time observing Bob as I could, and one day while hanging around the studio while Bob was on the air, I told him I was taking flying lessons. The conversation took a serious tone as Bob told me that flying might be a lot of fun, but it's a serious hobby. That thought has remained with me to this day.

Now for some lighter moments. In the radio business Bob was known to be a risk-taker. One day in 1972 while Bob was on the air, a national record promoter was visiting to promote the new Nilsson album, *Son of Schmillson.*

The promoter handed Bob the album, and without knowing anything about the album, Bob turned on the mike and announced that he had the new release from Nilsson.

He proceeded to put the album on the turntable. The promoter was frantically trying to warn Bob, but he proceeded and played the first cut. It started with these lyrics: "You're breaking my heart. You broke it apart so @#@# you!"

Bob immediately took the record from the turntable and turned red. He was speechless. I know that's hard to believe. This was before the shock radio of today.

Here are two of my most valued moments. I took Bob's lead and in 1973 I started to be a risk-taker in my own right. As a joke I started playing the "Monster Mash" over and over. For some reason we started to get some local interest in the former hit of 1963. From local interest it went national, sold a million copies, and WOKY was awarded the gold record.

Bob hated the record and took it off the wall at the radio station. He handed it to me and told me to take it home and put it on my wall. It remains there to this day.

As we all know, Bob was extremely competitive. In 1973 while at WOKY, Bob and I were sent to be in a George Washington birthday pie-eating contest at the Southgate Shopping Center in Milwaukee. The prize was a small plaque with the inscription: "I never met a cherry I didn't like."

Bob was determined to win. What Bob didn't figure on was that I would cheat him out of the prize he so desperately wanted. The three pies were placed in front of us. The bibs were in place and the whistle blew to start the contest. It was a timed event to see who could eat the most pie in a certain time.

While Bob was really eating the pies, I was faking it and throwing pie under the table. The judges didn't see me cheating, and I was awarded the top prize, the valued plaque.

For 12 years the plaque remained on my wall, then guilt set in. I took the plaque off the wall and sent it to Bob with a letter confessing to the cheating, that he was the real winner. Bob wrote back with a letter of his own: "You would cheat another disk jockey? Is there no honor? I'll get you for that!" Then he made me laugh again with his ending. "How's tricks?"

Getting Bob Back to Records

Joe Staudacher

Joe Staudacher is retired. He was a fixture at Marquette University's broadcasting department.

My radio name was Joe Landry. I used to get mail addressed to "Joe Laundry." I guess I didn't enunciate enough.

Bob was working at WOKY in about 1967, and he was doing the WOKY TOKY show, which ran every night from 11 p.m. to midnight, except Sunday when it was 10 p.m. to midnight. He wanted to get off that show and get on records in the afternoon.

So he called one of his friends, Sue Riordan from Marquette University in Milwaukee, and asked if she knew anybody who could help him out. I had been doing weekend and summer-vacation work at three or four other stations during the years I set up the broadcasting department at Marquette. So I was known around the university as doing a little work on radio, especially my jazz show on Saturday nights, 9 p.m. to midnight.

Sue recommended me to Bob. He called me up and said, "How would you like to do a session on remembering names?" That was a technique I taught in the Dale Carnegie course. I said that would be fine, but radio isn't the best way to do it because we need the pictures. He said, "Then how about talking on communications?" I couldn't turn that down.

I had my kids call in with good questions that I could answer. So these questions come in, and I'm answering them. I sounded really good. I didn't know that was my audition for the show.

The next night he took me down to an exclusive restaurant in Milwaukee and asked if I'd like to help him out and take over the show. That was it. With Bob everything was pretty straightforward. He either liked you or not.

I did that show for four months until they could get a full-time man in there to do news and the talk show. One night after I left the station, I was at home when the phone rang. It was Bob Collins on the line. He said, "I'm in love with your daughter. Is she home?" I had to laugh. He was always making you laugh that way.

I Apologized for What Bob Collins Said

Bernie Strachota

Bernie Strachota was president and general manager of WRIT and WBCS in Milwaukee. Retired, Strachota lives in Ocala, Florida. He is a member of the Wisconsin Broadcasters Hall of Fame.

During the 19 years I spent in broadcasting, I got to know that Bob was a very sensitive individual, which a lot of people didn't realize. He had a marvelous sense of humor.

We got Bob through George Wilson, who was the program director at WOKY. George and the people at WOKY had a parting of the ways. I was looking for a program director, and George Wilson was very controversial, very talented. He and Bob Collins were close associates. As a result of George coming to WRIT, we were fortunate enough to get Bob to join us.

Shortly after Bob started, I went to lunch with Bob and George. On the way back, George asked if I'd be willing to go on the air and apologize for what Bob Collins said on the air, and assure the audience that it would never happen again.

I said, yeah, I'll do that.

So the next day, I cut a quickie and said, "I apologize for what Bob Collins said on the air yesterday. I can assure you he did not express the sentiments of the station, and it will never happen again."

The switchboard lit up. Everyone wanted to know, "What did he say?" It was just a ploy. An audience-grabber. He never said a thing. This was a great idea of George Wilson's, and it worked. It got Bob Collins noticed.

Mike Drew, the *Milwaukee Journal* writer, called me and said, "Bernie, I don't blame you. You were right to say that. I want to quote it exactly, so tell me what Collins said."

I said, "Well, Mike, if you were listening, you heard what he said."

"Yeah," Mike said, "but I want to quote it exactly."

I think we said we didn't want to repeat it.

Bob never did say anything. He got a big kick out of the whole thing, though, because it caused quite a stir.

Our station grew from there, and we started an FM station. We were playing with different call letters. We had WFWO (We're For Women Only). Bob and I had a trailer, and the two of us sat there for hours, selecting music we could put on that particular station. It grew into a close friendship.

My wife and I built a new home in Brookfield, Wisconsin. We had the entire staffs of both stations out to our house. During the course of the evening, I was going to announce that I was promoting Bob Collins to vice president of programming. After I made that announcement, Bob got very excited and went off and had two quick toddies, then he got sick in our bathroom. He was actually a very modest guy.

My wife came to me and said, "If you ever do anything like this again, so help me there are going to be problems!"

He always called me Strachotudda, and I called him Booby. When he got the offer from WGN, he talked with me about it. I said, "Listen, Booby, you have a chance to go there, and by all means, you go. I know you're going to be a success. If it doesn't work out, the doors will always be open here."

We kept in close touch.

My all-time favorite story about Bob was this one: After I retired in 1986, a package arrives at home. It's from WGN radio. I open it up and there's a box of very nice golf balls. I said, "Can you imagine Collins sending these!" When I opened the box, they were the ugliest golf balls I'd ever seen—dirty, cuts on them, some yellow, some green. No card, nothing. That's the way he was!

I had a lot in common with Bob. I had been a fighter pilot in World War II and flew B-38s. That always intrigued Bob, that I was a pilot, and I think it got him involved in flying himself.

I never went flying with Bob, though. Just about six months before Bob died, I came back to Wisconsin to visit our children and grandchildren. Somebody said Bob was on the air and said, "I understand my old friend Bernie Strachotudda is visiting up in Wisconsin, and I'm going to go to a broadcasters luncheon." Whoever it was at WGN told him that he'd missed the broadcasters meeting. It was held the day before! Bob was so upset. Through Don Metzger, he found out where I was staying and gave me a call.

"I want to see you so badly," he told me. We got together that Saturday night in Milwaukee at the Grenadiers. We had an absolutely wonderful evening reminiscing. I said, "When are you going to fly down to Florida and spend some time with us?" Bob said, "I'm going to take you up on that, but you're going to have to fly with me when I get down there."

That's the last time we had a chance to talk to each other.

Picnics and Picking Music

Lee Rothman

Lee Rothman is vice president of the Milwaukee Broadcasters Club and a former co-worker of Bob Collins at WRIT.

Bob never acted like the important person he was. He didn't really feel important. I remember once we went for breakfast at Lou Mitchell's. In the cab, I said to Bob, "I don't know how you can handle all of this." And he said, "Handle what?"

"The attention," I told him. Bob looked around. "This guy, the cab driver, doesn't even know who I am," he told me. "You have to be on television in Chicago before anyone really notices you. I'm just a radio guy, I'm nothing. If they don't see you, it doesn't mean much."

Bob never went around talking about how great he was, or how great everything was for him. It was his job and he did it. That was his attitude. He told me the great joy for him was being able to meet important people. He loved that he got to know Cardinal Bernardin.

He was just an easygoing guy. That's what I remember about him from his days in Milwaukee. We both worked at WRIT, which at the time was a rock station. Then we got new owners and they changed its format. The new owners told Bob they didn't want a rock 'n' roll station anymore. They were turning it into nice songs. They told Bob that we would pick the music, records suitable for this new station.

Lee Rothman

Three times a week I would go to Bob's home in Oconomowoc, Wisconsin. We'd sit out at the lake having a couple of toddies, picking music. There we were having an actual picnic with a record player and tons of albums. We'd come back with our report.

I used to drive out to his house; it was about a 30-minute drive. Many a day I drove back, I wasn't sure where I was. It was always party time. In case anyone hasn't told you, Bob loved a good party.

If I had to put him into one sentence, I'd say Bob was a man's man. He loved the motorcycle, the airplane, traveling to places to see what's going on. He just lived life to the fullest.

Still, Bob was a very quiet kind of guy, too. He wanted people to know he was in good shape. He never wanted people to know if he needed help. I was told later there were times in his life that he was very down. He would never want you to know that.

He Was Like a Mature Big Brother

Robb Edwards

Robb Edwards is host of the morning show at WTMJ in Milwaukee.

I first met Bob Collins (Robert L.) in October of 1970 when I was hired by George Wilson to do the all night show on 1340 WRIT, Milwaukee. Bob was the afternoon-drive jock, the wild man, the guy who pushed the envelope as far as you could then. He was a guy who had been around, and I immediately looked up to him. Bob was the big brother I never had, a mentor, and ultimately a friend.

Shortly after I started there, Bob was named program director. He took me off nights and put me on middays, and then eventually into the morning show. And we had our moments. We got along wonderfully.

He was like a big brother. I was new to radio, having only worked in radio about two years. I admired him so much, and yet we conflicted. I was young and had all the answers, so we were butting heads all the time.

He taught me a lot of things. He taught me things I'll never forget about not only being in radio, but how to conduct yourself in life.

Bob, I think, was more educated, more mature, and much wiser than he ever let on. When my wife and I experienced some problems in our marriage, Bob helped us smooth things out. It was before he married Valerie Voss, the meteorologist who went to CNN.

When our second son was born, Bob was the guy who got up early and worked the morning show so I could be at the hospital. When he was appointed program director, he was the one I looked to for all the answers. Of course, there were many times we disagreed, but he always listened to my side of things first.

Bob, in fact, taught me two things I will always remember:

1. Always be yourself. Don't do what I do, do what I say. Some of us back then tried to be like him on the air, but we couldn't because he was best at what he did;

2. On your worst days you are never as bad as you think you are. And on days when you think you are amazing, you're not as good as you think you are. Keep that in mind and you'll be around for a long time!

Physically, he looked like a wild man. He was tall, about six-foot-one or -two and dripping wet he weighed maybe 160 pounds. He had long hair down to his shoul-

Robb Edwards

ders, with a big mustache. He looked like a typical hippie of the '70s.

Inside, he was very mature. He had gone to college and was learned. He knew what he was talking about.

He played this country-boy hick who got away with saying "damn" and "hell" on the radio anytime he could. People thought, "What a goof!" And he was much smarter than that. But he kept that persona. People really admired him.

He was always who he was. He never changed that persona. He quieted down after a while and wasn't so willing to push the envelope. But 30 years earlier, if you said "damn" and "hell" on the radio, you were getting away with a lot.

I've been in radio now 31 years. In that time I can count on one hand the guys who influenced me. He was one of them. I've carried his philosophies through my entire broadcasting career.

If you were lucky enough to be friends with or work with Bob Collins, you'll never forget him.

I'll never forget when Bob was the program director at WRIT. We had a meeting every now and then of all the people on the air. That always included air checks, which were a lot of fun. Bob didn't like to have meetings anyway. He wasn't in a particularly good mood this day. I think mine was the first and it was obviously lousy, so he was in a bad mood. We got to Jim Kagan, who had to read a tag line for one of the stories, Kohl's or Red Owl. Jim read the special of the week as something like "$2.49 for a gallon of bulk stool ice cream." I was so glad I heard the Bob Collins laugh before because I'll never forget it. Everytime I saw Bob Collins after that, I would always say, "Would you like to get together and go to the store and get some ice cream?" We'd always laugh about it.

Turns out it was a copywriter's mistake. It wasn't Jim Kagan's. The copy should have been "bulk style," but it was written "bulk stule." Jim read it like a pro. But "bulk stule" ice cream ended that meeting with the biggest laugh I can remember with Bob Collins.

A Big Laugh for Bob

Jim Kagan

Jim Kagan was a disk jockey at WRIT in Milwaukee.

I was working overnight. I worked the night shift for quite a few years.

So one day we're having a meeting, the first meeting, I think, after Bob took over as program director.

Here we were with this new crew. Bob was bringing tapes of all the shows.

He'd play the tapes and we'd hear how everyone did. So he plays my tape and starts laughing.

I said, "What's so bad?"

Bob says, "Did you hear what you just said?"

He played it again and I heard it; "bulk stool ice cream." Well, I heard it that time and I was shocked. "I can't believe I said that," I told Bob.

He starts laughing again.

He plays the tape again and everyone starts laughing. I had to laugh, too.

It was about the worst thing I had ever said on the radio. It actually came out on the air. It was unbelievable. I was very careful after that.

Tapping into People around Him

Leroy Wolniakowski

Leroy Wolniakowski is now retired and lives in Milwaukee.

I started at WRIT in 1965 as chief engineer. When Bob came in to do the afternoon show, I was his chief engineer. That's how I got to know him. We worked together in many different ways. He used to call the engineering department while we were on the air about one thing or another. He'd try to kid me.

At first I didn't know what to do because I wasn't used to that. Nobody knows you when you work in engineering.

If you remember, he did the same thing on WGN. He'd call Orion or some news guy or sports guy. Ask questions, get them involved.

In my 44 years in the broadcast business, he was the only one to include the engineers in his show. That was the unique thing about Bob. He knew how to tap into people around him to make his show more interesting.

I don't think it would surprise anybody to know that Bob had his own rules about how to do things. Whatever he wanted to do, he pretty much did.

There's no doubt that among all the people I've worked with, Bob was at the top.

Bob Never Had Much Fashion Sense

Judy Nest

Judy Nest lives in Moscow, Idaho. She's an associate professor at the University of Idaho.

I got a job at WRIT in my senior year of high school. They liked me so much when I would return in the summer from college, I'd go back there and work. I usually worked during the holiday breaks, too.

Bob was there the same time I was there.

There were about 40 full-time and 20 part-time workers there.

There was a receptionist who was very nice, but young. A little older than me by maybe five years. Bob would come in and stop at her desk each day. He'd say one of two things to her each day, either "Keep it" or "Burn it." This was in relation to her clothes.

She was going on vacation, and I needed to fill in at the reception desk. I busied myself in the mailroom so that I wouldn't be there when Bob walked in to comment on my clothes. But my timing didn't always work out. And when Bob would see me, he'd give the same "Burn it" or "Keep it" review.

Well, I did do something one time that sort of paid him back. When I think about it now, it's funny.

We had a Mag Card typewriter, which was like an IBM Selectric, except it had this little machine next to it. You would put a magnetic card inside of it similar in size and shape to the old computer punch card. This was kind of a pre-computer in the office.

At that time I was doing logs and correspondence for the salesmen. I got to use this typewriter. You would type a letter and you coded in stops, so when you wanted to do multiple letters, all you had to do was key in specific information. It was a form letter and saved a lot of time.

I was leaving for lunch one day and Bob asked if he could use that typewriter. I asked him if he knew how it worked and he said he did. I went off to lunch and when I came back he had been working on this document all during lunch. He said he was finally done and all he had to do was print it.

So he went to press "play" and it didn't do anything because he forgot to press "record" before he started. So he spent his entire lunch to do this letter and had to do it all over again.

It was fun talking about the days when both Bob and I worked at WRIT. It brought back lots of good memories for me and even Bob's demeanor at the time I worked with him taught me a little bit more about life.

Chapter 3

• • • • • • •

Milwaukee Friends

Bob Collins (top right) horsing around with his co-workers from WRIT in June 1972.

The Kid Who Lived in the Basement

Bob Pittman

Bob Pittman is the president of America Online.

Bob Collins gave me my first big break in the business, and I'll always remember that. I was a disc jockey at age 18, going to college in Jackson, Mississippi. I decided I wanted to break into the big time. I sent some audition tapes around the country to what I thought were the big stations.

One was WRIT in Milwaukee, and the program director was Robert L. Collins.

I was sitting at home one day off from school. The phone rang, and it was Bob Collins. He said he liked my tape and asked, "How'd you like to work summer swing, fill in for the summer?" I said, "Great. I'll be there. When?"

I packed my car, and headed out to Milwaukee.

I knew nothing, knew no one up there, didn't know how I was going to live, didn't have a place to live. Bob had moved into a house in West Allis, I think, and he said, "I have a waterbed in my basement; you can stay in my basement."

I lived with Collins and did not only summer swing, but as soon as I got there, some guy quit and went to Chicago, so I got a full-time job. If not for Bob, I would never gotten into the big markets.

The competing station, WOKY, had a sister station in Detroit, and about six months later the sister station offered me a job and off I went. Bob and I stayed good friends.

I wound up in Chicago at WMAQ as program director, doing the afternoon show around 1974-75. Bob came to WGN around the same time, and we were on opposite each other. We stayed friends.

When I was running Six Flags in Gurnee, I started coming to Chicago. I would come on Bob's show and talk about the new rides.

Bob and I did a motorcycle ride two or three years ago, rode out of Sun Valley, Idaho, down to Aspen, Colorado. We shared the love of motorcycles. We also shared a love of airplanes. Ironically, when I moved in with Bob in Milwaukee, he was not yet a pilot, but I was.

He had a great interest in flying and always talked with me about it. It was no surprise to me when he started lessons.

He was a dear friend and a wonderful guy.

I'll just tell you a little about myself. I was at WMAQ in Chicago and programmed the FM station WKQX. They sent me to New York for WNBC.

I was hired away by Warner to program their cable channels, including The Movie Channel. I later started MTV and was presi-

Bob Collins (far left) and Bob Pitman and his wife (far right)

dent of MTV networks. We sold the company to Viacom in 1985. I left in 1987, briefly did a stint with my own company, then went back to Warner, when they were merging with Time. I bought the Six Flags theme parks for Time Warner.

We sold Six Flags in 1995. I bought a piece of Century 21 Real Estate and ran that for a year. I was on the board of directors at America Online and then became the president and CEO of AOL.

Every time I went on Bob's show, he would tell everyone that I was the kid who lived in the basement, no matter what job I had. It made me laugh every time.

He was a good friend. If there was any bad press or anything weird, Bob would call up and give me a pat on the back, a little support.

Friend, Biker, Pancake-Lover

Tom Collins

Tom Collins has worked in Milwaukee as the voice of the Braves, Brewers, and Marquette basketball team. He is currently with WOKY in Milwaukee.

Robert L. Collins touched the lives of millions of people. Most of those knew him as simply "Uncle Bobby," that sometimes-funny guy on the radio at WGN, Chicago, in the morning. Controversial at times, abrasive at times, loved to talk about flying…motor-sickles (as he called them), da Bears, da Cubs, and his adopted hometown, Chicago! Conversant with staff members, he apparently respected them for their, as he would say, ex-per-teez!

My name is also Collins, no relation, and I'm also a radio guy and old enough to have children of my own who were his age! Though we worked in the same radio market (Milwaukee) for several years, we never really met, like perhaps trains that passed in the night—metaphorically, that is, as I'm sure there are those who would say we both had a love of the night and the lights!

I became a fan after he moved to Chicago to take over the morning show and replaced Wally Phillips, another Chicago radio icon. I had hosted a morning show here in Milwaukee for several years, as well as being known for my sports broadcasting. He became my morning elixir and our inevitable meeting happened up in Door County, in Wisconsin's Sister Bay, where we ironically had a

Tom Collins

mutual friend, Al Johnson, proprietor of the restaurant that boasted of its fine Swedish cuisine and proprietor of several rental properties. Bob, like myself, had remarried younger wives and the wives would politely listen to our usually brief conversations, usually dealt with our mutual respect of airplanes, motor-sickles, radio, mutual friends, and current (tasty) jokes.

For me, my icon, my dear friend, my fellow pilot, my fellow biker, he is on a sabbatical and, hopefully, we'll meet again and talk again, laugh again, and I'll say again, "Bob, you're crazy! And let's have one for the road."

Always Time for a Friend

Bryan McIntyre

Bryan McIntyre lives in Raleigh, North Carolina. He has managed radio stations in Columbus and Dayton, Ohio; Pittsburgh, Pennsylvania; Richmond, Virginia, and Raleigh, North Carolina. He now consults for pharmaceutical companies on media-based patient recruitment for clinical trials.

My best memories of Bob were when he was morning man/ program director of WRIT in Milwaukee in the early 1970s. He was a witty rock 'n' roll deejay then. I was just out of college and was fortunate enough to have gotten the program director's job at WCOL in Columbus, Ohio, a sister station of WRIT.

Bob was very gracious to this youngster, spending long hours on the telephone explaining how he did things in the "big city."

In those days he was known on the air as Robert L. Collins, and his unique sense of humor shone through the restrictive Top 40 format, which limited ad libs to less than 10 seconds. But because he was the program director he managed to bend his own rules a little.

In 1982, when I was out of work, he got me two major-market job interviews.

From 1985-91, I was general manager of WPTF, Raleigh's version of WGN, with 50,000 watts at 680 and the flagship of

North Carolina State University football and basketball. Up to this time I had only managed rock-music stations, and my challenge was to modernize the "old fashioned" programming of this very conservative, cautious station.

In 1986 I attended a broadcasting convention held in Chicago. I called Bob, and we arranged to meet in the lobby of the main hotel. When I arrived it was easy to find Bob; he was surrounded by about 50 people, a variety of local fans, old radio friends, and a number of high-profile national radio executives. When I caught his eye from the fringe of the crowd he yelled, "Bryan," and used me as an excuse to extricate himself from the mob. We got on one up elevator, got on a different down elevator, and found a table in a little coffee shop nearby where Bob sat with his back to the door so we could talk. For 30 minutes he gave what seemed like a hundred suggestions how I could make WPTF the kind of success that WGN was. Many of his ideas worked very well in Raleigh!

When I was in Chicago on business in the '80s and early '90s, he always took my calls. He was never too successful to forget an old friend. When I was fortunate enough to hear him on the radio, he was the same on the air as he was off. No phoniness, just human warmth. What a talent!

An old radio friend mailed me two cassettes of WGN's programming on the night following Bob's death. I knew Bob had become a Chicago institution, but what I heard on those tapes gave me a much better sense of how much Chicago loved Bob.

A Teenager at Heart

Dick Ginkowski

Dick Ginkowski is a state prosecutor in Kenosha, Wisconsin, who worked in Milwaukee radio.

I was known as Dick Scott, and I worked in radio in Kenosha, Racine, Waukesha (WAUK), and Milwaukee (WISN). "Robert L." (he wasn't known as "Bob" until WGN) was a somewhat renegade rock-'n'-roll jock who had a penchant for being politely irreverent.

He was like a teenager who grew slightly older—not that this is a particularly bad thing. When he was hired at WGN, it was like an earthquake—something akin to going to a microwave cookoff wearing a pacemaker.

Robert L. was the least likely person to invade the staid confines of 2501 West Bradley Place. He did, however, eventually charm over even the most skeptical, and, like most of us, he became a bit more conservative over the years. Nonetheless there was still the teenager in him who fueled his sense of humor. He did slow down when he married Christine, who appeared to be a major influence in his life. Before that, he was very much in the fast lane, but that was not uncommon for broadcast people of the time.

The operative word is "of the time," because the chances that another person with original wit and character will arise today are slim. Corporate broadcasting has led to a proliferation of rather boring and generic (unless they are shocking) broadcast "personalities" (I use that term loosely).

Robert L., like me, got his start at 13 (they got sick of seeing me hanging around the radio station so I got a job), and the rest is history. I got out and got a paying job. He stayed in and was lucky enough (and talented enough) to get an even better-paying one. (I was a newsperson, and generally the trade-off is that news people used to have more longevity in the business.)

The hoopla over his death was embarrassing, and certainly he would have felt that way. Yes, it was a legitimate news story, but it was milked far too much. What happened at the hospital in Zion was a major news story even if some "nobody" was involved. Unfortunately the coverage got turned a bit from that to his death. The fact that two other people were killed and a ball of flame shot down a hospital hallway was downplayed.

A Secret Packer Fan!

Bill Broege

Bill Broege lives in West Bend, Wisconsin. He is retired from Columbia Records.

When Bob was a young rock-'n'-roll disk jockey in Milwaukee, I worked with Columbia Records, out of both Milwaukee and Chicago. We had parties for the artists who were in Milwaukee, and that's where my association started with Bob.

Lots of new artists came through Milwaukee, and they all met Bob at these parties: Billy Joel, Pearl Jam, Meat Loaf, Bruce Springsteen, Liza Minnelli. We would do concerts in Milwaukee, Madison, Green Bay, anywhere in the Wisconsin market.

We even had a party on a boat one time in Milwaukee. I remember Bob was an avid boater at the time.

Later, when I was working in Chicago and Bob was with WGN, I'd meet him for lunch or a beer, sometimes with Jimmy Brown, who was a friend of Bob from his Milwaukee days. The thing about Bob was that he never forgot his friends.

In the radio business, there are always shenanigans going on. But not with Bob. He was always above-board. Although he was somewhat of a rebel, he still was very honest and sincere.

I remember one story about Bob. It involves Jim Scully, who was Ron Riley's brother. Now Jim also worked for Columbia records. Ron Riley worked for WLS in the '60s. He was a huge name in Chicago radio. At one time, though, Ron Riley was Smiley Riley at WOKY.

Jim had an in with NFL Films, and Bob was a big Bears fan. He was also a Packer fan, unbeknownst to many. And I was an avid Packer fan. Jim got us TV passes to the Packer-Bear game on a Monday night.

Being a Chicago personality now, Bob sat with the Bears, although I always thought he secretly would have come over to the Packer bench. He knew better than that!

Well, I saw Bob across the field behind the Bears bench, and I decided to walk across the field and say hello. Well, inadvertently I walked in front of the punter as he was practicing. I nearly caught the ball in my face. I thought Bob was going to die laughing. He was that kind of guy. And when he started laughing, he'd have everyone around him laughing.

He Could Talk about Everything

Larry Johnson

Larry "The Legend" Johnson worked in radio in both Milwaukee and Chicago.

I was a part-time guy from Milwaukee doing a show at WGN in Chicago.

I used to fly in and do Wally's show on WGN when Wally went on vacation. It would be a week or two weeks at a time. When I'd get back to Milwaukee, people would always tell me they heard me on that radio. It's amazing how many people listened to that morning show on WGN.

I first met Bob when I was doing Wally's show. I had a ball with him. He'd come in and ask about the Milwaukee guys, what was happening around town, stuff like that. He'd talk to you about just about everything.

I appreciated how much Bob changed over the years. I don't mean his personality, but the way he worked on the radio. When he started, he was pretty crazy. But later on he had such maturity. Just about everybody who listened to him, no matter what age they were, could get something out of his show.

He was such a pro. I idolized him.

Not an Opera Kind of Guy

Jonathan Green

Jonathan Green has been on Milwaukee's WTMJ since 1969. He lives on Okauchee Lake in Wisconsin, is married with three sons and two grand-daughters, and is also an avid Harley rider.

I knew Bob in the early 1970s in Milwaukee, where I have been afternoon drive with AM-620 WTMJ. He was a rock jock and program director with both WOKY and WRIT. He had tried to get me to go to work for him, and that's how we became acquainted.

When I met Bob he lived in a rented house on a lake with a boat, and I thought that was very special. He moved away for a while, and when he came back he lived in another lake home! That was too much for me. I just had to follow, so in 1972 I bought a lake home 30 miles west of Milwaukee near where Bob's second place was. I believe he had moved to Chicago by then. I still live there.

Another connection was Valerie, who ultimately became Bob's second wife.

She was his girlfriend when we met, but he had broken up with her. I dated her in 1972, but she couldn't get past her infatuation with Bob. The rest is, as they say, history.

My last social experience with Bob was about 10 years ago. I had manipulated a pair of tickets to the Chicago opening of *Phantom of the Opera*, and planned to meet Bob and Chris at their house and then go on into Chicago for dinner and the show.

My wife Kathy and I arrived at their house only to find

Jonathan Green

Bob in cut-off shorts and a dirty T-shirt cleaning his eight-car garage. He'd changed his mind!

Well, after a tour of the property, we had to press on without them. I was disappointed, of course, but understandably that was just Bob's style.

Frankly, had I not been enamored with *Phantom,* I'd have preferred working around my home as well.

My enduring impression of Bob Collins is my admiration of the way he worked within an industry filled with big egos and considerable leverage. He pushed right through and was given his due without overplaying the ego card.

He did it his way, without being intimidated, and was neither hated nor envied for it, but rather admired for his ability to accomplish it.

I wish I had been able to do that.

Spinning Records on a Sunday Afternoon

Pat Martin

Pat Martin is publisher of TV Business Confidential. *He owns WMOM radio.*

In 1970, I had come to Milwaukee to attend a Rod Stewart concert. I was a little early, and I went to the back door of a radio station. I went downstairs, and they let me in, Sunday afternoon. There was this guy sitting behind the control board spinning records. It was Bob Collins.

I asked him why he wasn't using cart machines, and he said, "Our program director, George Wilson, believes we should use records. You're not disc jockeys unless you're using records." I said, "It makes some sense to me."

See, radio stations by then were using a tape cartridge, three by four inches. He was actually spinning records. Most of the stations had switched to dubbing records onto these tapes. The record vinyl would break down after about 50 plays, and they'd have to replace the records constantly.

He had a rack where two turntables were sitting. Eleven years later I became program director of that station and wound up getting the rack, which is still being used at my radio station today. It's ironic I would meet him in 1970 this way, and then 11 years later become program director at WRIT.

In 1984, I was managing a station, and we conducted something called The Outrageous Contest. People came up with ideas of what they would do to win a seven-carat sapphire. Bob interviewed us on the air. He loved contests like that. I think he thought it brought out the best and worst in people.

Southern Boy, Sharp as a Tack

Tom Shanahan

Tom Shanahan was friends with Bob Collins in Milwaukee. A veteran of more than 50 years in radio, Tom worked as an announcer, program director, and station manager at WEMP, Milwaukee. He worked many public appearances with Bob, who was a friendly competitor. He is now on the air daily at WTKM in Milwaukee. Shanahan's "Club 60" program features a nostalgic blend of popular music.

When Bob lost his job at WRIT, he popped in to see me and said, "Hey, you always said you'd have a job for me." I was program director at WEMT, and I said, "Bob, honestly, we are totally overstaffed. I can't add anybody."

I remember telling him, "You know, you don't have to be program director. You can make it as a deejay. You've been program director at WOKY and WRIT, you've been a deejay in the past. You can continue to be successful." So I said, "Go that route."

He took a job in Kansas City and, meanwhile, Paul Gallis was recommending him highly to the management at WGN. Bob came in, did the audition, and got the job. That was absolutely super.

I heard that audition when they played it on WGN after his death. The audition was very revealing. It showed what a terrific personality he was. Usually when you do an audition, you're tense,

Tom Shanahan

you're very, very straight. But he was loose and doing it in the Bob Collins style.

His style was very relaxed. He was very well-informed and had a great sense of humor. He was in command. He sounded like a Southern boy who didn't know too much, but when you got right down to it, he was sharp as a tack.

Every day for years, Bob Collins started the day right for Chicagoans and Midwesterners on WGN. He became a great interviewer, and it didn't matter if it was the president of the United States, the governor of Illinois, the mayor of Chicago, or just plain Joe Six Pack.

One time he came up to see me. We had a condo in Kohler, Wisconsin. When Bob was building his house, he rode his motorcycle up to Kohler. We had dinner. He looked at the fixtures of the Kohler company. I asked why he wanted to visit the Kohler company, and he said they made good stuff, and then he said he heard that the Irish invented the toilet seat. There was a slight pause, then Bob said, "Ten years after the Irish invented the toilet seat, the Germans invented the hole in it."

That's when I saw his bike. It was fantastic. He loved that bike. He just dug that sort of thing. He liked all that kind of stuff. That's why he had a plane. And he didn't just have any old kind of plane; he had an acrobatic plane.

Bob Collins maintained his friendship with countless Milwaukee broadcasters, and all of us share the sense of loss with his Chicago colleagues at WGN, with countless listeners and fans, and with his family and his wonderful wife, Christine.

Chapter 4

· · · · · · ·

WGN Years

Roy Stanek

Sammy Kahn and Bob Collins

"I Got Just the Guy for You"

Paul Gallis

Paul Gallis was a friend of Bob Collins for many years. He recommended Bob to the folks at WGN.

I met Bob Collins in Milwaukee when I was doing record promotions. He was a disk jockey at WOKY, and he used to also work at WRIT. That was in the late '60s and early '70s.

Paul Gallis

He had some confrontation with George Wilson, who was his general manager in Milwaukee. It wasn't a serious argument, but George wasn't the kind of guy who let anyone else run the station. Bob was the kind of guy who did the programming he thought he needed to do. George wanted to help some record people, and Bob didn't think so.

Well, as luck would have it, I was sponsoring a national meeting around this time, bringing people from different stations around the country to Chicago. Bob Henley from WGN came to one of those meetings.

Henley asked me to come to his office and talk. He wanted my opinion, comparing WGN to other stations in the area. I told him it had a older sound, that it appealed to an older audience. Well, Henley told me the station wanted to make a change.

Not long after that, I was walking through the halls at WGN and I passed Bob Henley's office. He called me in and said, "Paul, we're looking for somebody for the afternoon slot. We need a younger guy."

Bob Collins was working weekends in Kansas City at a radio station. I told Henley, "I got just the guy for you." I always thought Bob was a phenomenal talent. When he worked in Milwaukee, he was number one in his slot. Henley said, "Get me a tape as soon as you can."

I called Bobby. He sent me a rock 'n' roll tape. I called him back and said, "Idiot, this is a 50,000-watt clear channel talk station, and they play music, but you don't need Tutti Frutti on the tape. You know what I mean?" I told him to give me a little more talk.

He got me a new tape the very next day, and I took it over to Bob Henley. They flew Collins in for a Saturday afternoon, live audition. They hired him on the spot.

If you ask me what my impression of Bob was, I'd tell you the same thing I told his mother at his funeral, and she said I was right. He was a hillbilly from Florida who was articulate and funny, knew how to use a double entendre, and was one of the best talents I ever heard. He could knock the hell out of Larry Lujack, Don Imus, and all of the other big names in radio.

Bob stayed at my house every weekend when he first came to Chicago. One day, he said to me, "Paulie, I need help." He had been showing up in everyone else's time slot, and I told him he had to stop that. "When the ratings come out, you're not going to have any for yourself," I told him. "Do just Wally Phillips' and Roy Leonard's time slots."

Whenever he introduced me, he'd say, "This man changed my way of living."

That was nice of him to say.

Fooling Around on the Radio

Dan Fabian

Dan Fabian is a former WGN general manager and program director.

"Bob Collins in 500 words or less." Uh-huh. No problem. Piece of cake. Can of corn. Two minutes of copy for a 60-second spot. And in the space left over I believe I'll whip off an ode to Allan Greenspan in archaic Celtic pentameter. The logical knee-jerk was to just dust off yet another funny story and smile and get back to trying to figure out how to kickstart mornings without a fix of that goofy, infectious cackle. Like anyone else who ever came within ten feet of the man, I have more than a few. The Taste of Chicago aerobics demonstration during which he involuntarily demonstrated his beached turtle impression. Or the time he explained how it was that chocolate doughnuts were okay with one of his dozen annual diets because he had already pouted through a grapefruit. Or his mild-mannered suggestion to the little kid in charge of Bozo's gong during the first and last "Pop Quiz" spelling bee final, or that San Francisco trip, or Ned Locke's retirement party. Well, no, not the last three, but you get the idea.

Then it dawned. While there is obviously no way to do justice to a fascinating, complex, multi-talented, and so on alleged adult in 500 words, "less" is doable. Many less, in fact. One, to be exact.

Friend.

If Bob was not the best of those I ever had, he was surely in the top three. Which did not exactly make me a member of the world's most exclusive club. The man had more best friends than he could count. Of the myriads of warm 'n' fuzzy memories—some of them almost accurate—smiled and cried over since the day the laugh died, the most uniquely defining was his amazing knack for making darned near anyone feel like a lifelong crony in 10 minutes flat and staying that way until further notice.

Maybe that was because of his voracious appetites for life and everything that came with it. Or the fact that he really loved those he loved and really enjoyed the things he enjoyed. And said so, right out loud, repeatedly. Or his uncanny ability to listen and actually hear. Or his generosity or street smarts or professionalism or head smarts or refined tastes in music or everyman tastes in everything else or the fun or maybe/probably/definitely that he never forgot who he was.

I met Bob Collins when he had a 34-inch waist and 12 bucks in his pocket and more hair on the top of his head than the bottom. We were still trading lines, threatening lunch, and having not one nightmare clue we were actually saying good-bye when we said it with only four days left on the clock.

He was the same guy.

I was in the room when a nasally, politically incorrect, closer-to-Johnny-Fever-than-Roy-Leonard audition tape convinced a genius named Bob Henley to bite hard and offer him a whopping $32,000 for a six-day-a-week, two-shows-a-day airshift that would have exhausted a Grand Canyon mule. And when he jumped at what any self-respecting media type or close-cover-before-striking school of broadcasting or competitor—especially competitor—would have happily explained at your slightest expression of interest was the utterly, totally, ridiculously impossible challenge of replacing the legit legend, Wally Phillips. And when he tried (and failed) to look cool signing his first seven-figure contract. We celebrated at Roma's. He bought. No surprises there. Case closed. The same guy.

The same simply—not to be even close to confused with simple—great friend who helped me through some very tough personal times and let me think I returned the favor once or twice. The one with whom, though I'm not sure either of us ever completely bought into the notion of radio being as much business as ultimate game, I grew up in business. The stone pro who could be steely-eyed tough and demanding and occasionally downright surly when it came to doing the job right, but who never lost sight of the fact he was paid to do for a living what most people pay to do for kicks.

Whenever someone asked, as someone invariably did, what the two-inch-tall, Cub Scout-carved "FAOTR" smack on the middle of his desk stood for, he would say, if he rightly remembered what the mantra meant, it was an acronym for his job. For just "Fooling Around on the Radio." Then he would allow as how that particular translation came "close enough!" Then he would laugh! And so would you.

And then the conversation would turn to today's show or tomorrow's show or the station or politics or airplanes or his review of the terrifically well-written articles in *Sports Illustrated*'s swimsuit issue or his new toy or old friends or family. And then he would say it was time to call Chris. And you would leave looking forward to doing it all again tomorrow.

Don't we all wish.

There are holes in a lot of top-three lists these days.

The Guy Who Hired Bob

Bob Henley

Bob Henley is the former general manager and program manager of WGN radio. He hired Bob Collins at WGN. Collins and Henley remained close after Henley moved to Sacramento in 1978 to manage radio stations.

As Collins would say when he would go on remote once in a while and I was along: "If you want to blame somebody, there's the guy. He did it."

The story about getting Bob is this. I was program manager at the time and my assistant was Dick Jones. We were in the midst of conducting an extensive search for an afternoon person, and we had listened already to somewhere between 200 and 250 tapes.

At that time, the WGN studios were still located on Bradley Place. We were working in Studio B Control. Dick would randomly select a tape from a box that held about 50 tapes. He would hand it to the engineer who would thread it up and hit "play." We'd listen to it until we couldn't take it anymore, then he'd put another one on.

We had worked our way through 25 or 30 tapes when we put on one that started out with rock 'n' roll music, certainly not the music of choice of WGN. When the music came to the end, on came this guy with a pretty unusual voice. He identified himself and gave the call letters of the station.

They were doing some type of on-the-air contest like Dialing for Dollars or Lucky Bucks, where they would call a telephone number and see if the person could answer a question. So Collins says, "Allright now, it's time to play, Lucky Bucks, and the call to-day goes out to—well, we'll just dial it up."

So he dials the number, we hear a couple of rings, when the operator cuts in and says: "What number are you calling?"

He gives her the number and she says, "Well, I'm sorry, that number has been disconnected."

Bob says, "Aw, I'm sorry to hear that. What are you doing, operator?"

Surprised, she answers, "I beg your pardon?"

Collins says again, "What are you doing?"

She answers, "Well, I'm working."

Collins says, "Well, have you got time to play Lucky Bucks?"

Jones looked at me. I looked at him and I said, "You can stop the tape. There he is."

And that's as simple as it was. He was confronted with a situation he didn't expect and didn't get flustered, and he turned it into something that was probably more interesting than if he'd connected with the number he called. He took a lemon and made lemonade.

So he was hired, even though there was some opposition to it.

Remember, this was in the '70s and WGN was still in the mode of the big-voiced announcers such as Carl Greyson and John Mallow, and personalities like John Doremus and Jay Andres.

Bob's voice didn't come close to what the typical WGN listener might expect. There was some well-placed opposition about hiring him. The quote was: "He doesn't sound like us." But Jones and I were pretty adamant about it. "The guy's fresh and he'll fit in," we said. "Give him a chance."

It was Jones' idea that we team Bob up with Greyson. Carl had the great, big, deep booming voice, and their shtick was for Carl to come out with some big, ponderous statement. Then Collins would cut him to ribbons in about three seconds. It clicked. And the listeners loved it.

A Typical Bob Collins Job Interview

Tom Petersen

Tom Petersen is the news director at WGN radio. Tom's comments were made at the Milwaukee Broadcasters Association tribute to Bob Collins.

I used to walk into the office before the show in the morning and Bob would look up at me and say, "Tom, what if we really had to work for a living? You don't realize how lucky we are."

Bob did realize how lucky he was. At the same time, he was one of the most talented individuals, one of the fastest minds, one

Tom Peterson and Lt. Col. John Cheyne, then Commander of the Chicago Chapter of the Salvation Army

Roy Stanek

of the funniest people you'd ever want to meet. In the later years as he got into being the Wally successor in Chicago, he really did become a tremendous interviewer and a man who got into a lot of issues and did them well.

The reason I got my job over at WGN was because of Bob, and it also had to do with Milwaukee. When I got there, the day I was supposed to interview for the job, I went to the news director's office, and he said, "I'll hire you because I like you, I think you're good. But Bob Collins has to like you."

No pressure there, you know.

He said, "We're waiting for Bob. He'll be here in just a few minutes." Well, Bob comes strolling in and shouts, "Hey, how are you?" Slaps me on the back and says, "Come on, we're going to go for a ride."

I get in the car with Bob. He had to renew his driver's license. We're driving in his Corvette, driving to the Illinois Secretary of State's office. Along the way he's telling me what a bad day he had. He gets to the point where he asks, "By the way, where were you before?"

I said, "Well, I was in Milwaukee the same time you were. I don't know if you remember me."

"Oh, yeah," he says. That's the last we said about broadcasting. He gets to the Secretary of State's office, gets whatever he needs, we get back in the car, tear back to the station, we walk into the news director's office, and he says, "He's from Milwaukee; he's got to be good."

And that was it.

He also used to like to intimate you a little bit. Early on we used to have the newsroom down on the first floor and the studios were on the second floor on Bradley Place. In order to get from the newsroom to the second floor you would literally have to run up two flights of stairs, halfway across the building, run into the news booth, and you'd be out of breath.

Bob would see you coming. It would be 2 o'clock. He'd never hit a newscast on time, except if you were out of breath. And I would run in, sit down in the chair, and he'd say, "And now the news; here's Tom."

Then he'd just sit there and go, "So, whatya gonna do?"

It was great. We had some tremendous times. He will be missed. As Paul Harvey said, "You can't replace Bob," but you've got a good guy in Spike O'Dell.

Paul Harvey

Roy Stanek

Uncle Bob Remembers Uncle Bobby

Bob Baron

Bob Baron was Uncle Bob on Lunchtime Little Theater on WGN-TV in the 1950s. He is a board member of AFTRA and a council member of the Screen Actors Guild. He is a past chair of the Betty Mitchell Sick and Benefit Fund. He's now retired and lives in La Grange Park, Illinois.

Betty Mitchell was a wonderful woman in Chicago. She was the membership secretary of the local AFTRA chapter in Chicago, and she helped actors and others in the business whenever she could. So when the board decided we ought to do something to help our members, we decided to name our sick and benefit fund in her honor.

Chicago is the only local to have a sick and benefit fund for its performers. In the old days, actors didn't have pensions and benefits. If they got sick, they were on their own.

I became chair of that committee and we needed some funds. So I decided to ask for help, and Bob Collins was one of the people who helped us. This was in 1984.

The restaurant, Boul Mich, said we could use its facility. One of the owners used to be an actor, so he knew what we were trying to do. We got talent from all around Chicago.

Bob Baron

Bob Collins came with Roy Leonard. Well, they were just marvelous. They were just the kind of local stars we needed to draw people to buy tickets and support our fund.

Bob especially was terrific, a fun guy. He had such an infectious laugh, a funny laugh. He went over big. Of course, so did Roy. They worked very well together, like they were a professional team. Nothing rehearsed, just ad libs. Lots of laughs. Some people can do that, just bounce off one another.

We made a lot of money that night. Thanks to those two, we had money to help our members pay their rent, pay hospital bills, things like that.

I'll always remember Bob Collins for that. And Roy. Always willing to help out.

The Ordinary Guy and Practical Joker

Roy Leonard

Roy Leonard has been a fixture in Chicago radio since the 1960s. He worked closely with Bob Collins at WGN and introduced him to Chicago audiences.

I was working a split shift at WGN, on the air from 10 to noon and then from 1 to 2 p.m. We heard they hired this new guy. We frankly knew nothing about him. Bob was a big star in Milwaukee, but we really didn't know anything about him in Chicago.

People cannot believe this, but outside of Chicago, WGN doesn't mean anything. It's a huge station, but outside of the individual markets you're really not that well-known. The same was true for Bob.

The thing I most remember that first day he walked into the station to start his job is that I asked him, "What would you like me to tell people about you?" Here I was going to be telling our audience about this new guy. He could have told me anything to say, to help set him up.

And he said, "Please say anything you wish." Now, that's very unusual. Ordinarily you'd expect somebody to give you a setup.

But not Bob. He was a very honest guy. What you heard on the radio was really him. There was nothing phony about him.

He was immediately warm to me. He always had a smile, he looked directly at you when he talked with you. He didn't have a problem with what you were going to say about him.

Roy Leonard

When he moved to mornings, my show followed his. It was so great to follow him because he had this huge audience. You're awfully lucky in our business to have that. Placement on the air is a very important thing. To be able to follow a guy like Collins just gave you this built-in audience, which you have to be thankful for.

His knowledge of music was amazing. He grew up in the middle of the rock 'n' roll era, while I got out of music in 1965 or 1966, right after the Beatles. There was a whole 10 years when I didn't pay attention to what was going on musically, because I wasn't involved. So I would ask him questions. If I heard a record and didn't know who was singing, you could ask Bob and he'd know right away. His knowledge of music was wonderful, and he didn't mind sharing that, which is nice.

There's a famous story about Bob and me, and it's a good one. He and Jim Loughman were on in the afternoons then. I was doing my split shift. And it was St. Patrick's Day. I don't remember exactly what they had to do. They had to either be at the beginning of the parade to kick it off, or they were riding on a float, but Bob said, "Look, Roy, you normally get off at 2, but would you stick around for about a half an hour, 'cause we'll be back. We can't get back by 2, but we'll get back by about 2:30." And I said, "Sure."

Well, I had plans for later in the day, so I really wanted to get out of there. When 2:30 came, they didn't show. When 3 o'clock came, they didn't show. And I began to be worried. I really wondered if they were all right. Finally, my producer and I started calling bars to see if we could find out where these guys were. They never came back. I worked 'til 4 or 5 o'clock.

Our program director at the time, Lorna Gladstone, says to this day that it's the first time she ever saw me appear to be angry. I'm one of those guys who has a naturally sunny disposition. I'm a pretty easy guy.

I figured out it had all been a setup. The next day they came in, laughin' and scratchin'. I remember I looked them in the eyes, and then I started laughing, too. You couldn't really get mad at Bob.

Every time I turn the radio on now, he isn't there. I miss him. I think we all do and we all will for a long time.

He was My Go-To Man

Spike O'Dell

Spike O'Dell is the new morning man on WGN, replacing Bob Collins. Spike's comments were made at the Milwaukee Broadcasters Association tribute to Bob Collins.

Somebody said that old Bobby never forgot his past.

My first week at WGN I got called upstairs to the 19th floor. And I'm thinking, "Man, have I screwed up? I've only been in town for a week." I went upstairs and I had to wait for about 15 or 20 minutes. Finally the secretary said the boss would see me.

So I walked in there and he said, "Are you O'Dell?" And I said, "Yeah."

And he said, "Don't forget where you came from."

Bob must have gotten that same speech because he didn't forget where he came from. He always spoke highly of Milwaukee.

Bobby was very, very good to me. I have fond memories. When I first got to WGN, he was the one who put his arm around me and told me what was the right thing to do, whom to stay away from, who were the good people, the bad people, a direction to go. As I've told so many people, I've kind of lost my go-to guy.

When there was so much crap flying around, when you didn't know who was telling you the truth, or what was up, when I couldn't figure it out myself, I'd say, "Okay, Bobby. Whatdya think?" And he'd tell me.

He was a mentor. And he had a terrific sense of humor.

When he'd call me in the morning, I'd be sitting there in my underwear and he'd always leave me with a question that made me squirm. He'd ask you

Christine Collins and Spike O'Dell

a question just to see how you were going to wiggle out of it. Well, Bobby, if you're listening today, you're still making me squirm because I don't know how you did this morning thing so well for so long. It's a juggling act. I've been doing it since the accident, and I'm still not used to it.

I have a lot of awe for him and how he did it. I'm just very impressed. I miss him, but he's always in our thoughts and in our lives. When I think of him, I smile, and I think that's the best thing you can say.

How Lucky to Have Bob as a Friend

James C. Dowdle

James C. Dowdle is a retired executive vice president of the Tribune Company. These remarks were taken from the eulogy he delivered at Bob Collins' funeral.

You can clearly tell what an impact this man had on the lives of the people here in Chicago.

For many of us, the first voice we heard in the morning and often the first laugh we shared came from this special man.

How lucky we were to have Bob Collins as a friend.

Each of us has been touched by him in a special way. He let people know what was going on. He took on the issues that mattered in his own thoughtful way. He always seemed to ask the right questions, the ones that were on the minds of the listeners.

Bob really didn't think of himself as a journalist. He always called himself a disc jockey. He started spinning 45s on the air when he was just 14 years old. And anyone who listened to his show knows Bob's fondness for the classics.

Who can forget songs like "Dead Skunk in the Middle of the Road." Or "Grandma Got Run Over By a Reindeer." And "The Yacht, Lyle Dean."

As you can tell from his play list, Bob didn't have many bad days. I was known as Mr. Doodle. One day somebody asked me, "Doesn't it bother you that Bob calls you Mr. Doodle on the air all the time?" I said, "No, not at all. You have to understand the spirit in which it's said. In fact, I really would worry if Bob ever called me Mr. Dowdle."

You never had to wonder what was on Bob's mind; he would always tell you. I had some interesting lunches with him over the years. Of course, these were business lunches, so he would wear his formal T-shirt.

At times we might disagree, but we had great, mutual respect for each other.

But then, Bob had great respect for everyone, especially those he worked with. Each morning he would engage the people around him, seeking information and opinions. He was the father of the morning team at WGN, and played off the people in the studio, always done in a good-natured way and always with respect.

It seemed like Bob knew everyone in town. We were all part of his life, and that meant we were part of his daily program, which is probably why he never really had to worry too much about planning what he had each day. His show was about all of us and what happened to us in Chicago.

He developed a special relationship with senators, governors, and the mayor. Their appearances on the show were always fascinating exchanges. Bob would never compromise his point of view, but you could tell, even with these high-ranking officials, that they were comfortable with Bob Collins.

There was never a trick question, and even when Bob didn't agree with them on a particular issue, there was always respect.

Make no mistake; there were definitely things Bob didn't like to do.

He hated ties. And he hated tuxedos. But he would wear them when it meant something important for the station or for a friend.

He emceed Governor Edgar's inauguration, hosted Governor Ryan's New Year's Eve party, and did many appearances for WGN, even if it meant wearing a tuxedo and a tie.

Oh, how this man loved Chicago, and that's not easy for a kid from Florida.

He became an integral part of this community. Just ask the folks at the Salvation Army. He believed in their mission and he never wavered from his support.

Planes, motorcycles, and automobiles. Bob Collins had so many cars, he qualified as a dealer. When I drove into the parking lot each morning, I always made a point to check his parking space just to see what was new in the cars.

Now Bob never met a meal he didn't like. He had such a petite figure. We would talk at length about diets and exercise. And Christine would try to help. She would pack his lunch with carrot sticks and fruit, but, as you know, Christine, Bob's palette ran more toward sliders and Italian beef. So he would secretly share his healthy lunch with his staff so he could save room for comfort food.

Bob loved comfort food, like doughnuts, chili dogs, moon pies, and even an occasional Jack Daniels.

He also loved comfort clothing, like suspenders, the big, blue handkerchief, and baseball caps. He wore these, because as he often reminded us on the air, he had only three hairs left on the top.

Christine was more than his partner. She was and always will be Bob's soul mate. She got up with him in the middle of the night when it was time for both of them to go to work. He left for the radio station. She went about the business of managing their home. They did so much together. They even rode his and her Harleys.

And, as I understand it, it was Christine who named the dog Booger so Bob could talk about it without getting into trouble.

Christine, nobody will miss Bob more than you. Such great love and devotion you had for each other. I know that Christine and

Bob Collins in a suit!

Bob often traveled together. With Bob, it wasn't so much the destination as it was the journey.

Flying gave him so much enjoyment. He shared this restless passion with another aviator, Charles Lindbergh, whose epitaph reads, "I shall take the wings of the morning and fly to the outermost ends of the sea."

And so it is with our fallen friend. Chicago will miss you Bob. Your humor, your insight, your help. And as you might have said to each of us if you had the chance, "So long, partner."

A Great Broadcaster, a Great Friend

Stephen Carver

This statement was released by Stephen Carver, vice president and general manager of WGN radio, following Bob Collins' death.

Bob Collins was the best-known part of the WGN family, but he was also part of the families and daily lives of millions of WGN listeners, in Chicago and throughout the country. As we feel great sadness at the loss of a friend and colleague of 25 years, we recall both the warmth and the fun he bought to the radio.

Bob Collins was as successful and respected as he was because he created a one-to-one relationship with each of us. He was a trusted friend and a great communicator, someone who related to us without an ounce of pretension.

He enjoyed life and had a passion for his family, his friends, his hobbies, and his favorite charities. We will remember Bob as part rebel and part teddy bear—a thoughtful voice who was always involved in his community. He was a great broadcaster and a true friend.

"Give Me the Script and Let's Do It!"

Mike Houlihan

Mike Houlihan is president of Mike Houlihan Creative in Chicago. He is also a writer, actor, and playwright.

I thought he was a cracker. He didn't sound very Chicago. He sounded like he was from the South. So I asked him to be in the Illinois State Fair Preview when I was doing special events for the State of Illinois Center.

This was when Thompson was governor. We had hog callers and husband callers and he was perfect to introduce them all.

He was a nice guy. Big, burly guy. He didn't need to prepare much. He was laid back, walked up, said, "Give me the script and let's do it." I gave him the script, and as he read the script on stage, he would read one page, crumple it, and throw it over his shoulder. I thought that was an interesting approach! It must be what he did on radio.

I only worked with him that one time. I listened to him once in a while, usually if I knew someone was going to be on. Or if I was plugging something.

There was no bullshit with this guy. He seemed like just your average Joe, just a guy who liked to eat and drink a lot. He liked to ride his motorcycle, simple pleasures, just like me.

Bob Collins: His Television Days

Al Hall

Al Hall is a consulting producer for WGN-TV. He was the producer/director for several television specials that featured Bob Collins.

We hired a guy from the West Coast to be a performer and consultant on Bozo. He had a lot of ideas, and one of them was to do a show with Bob Collins. This was a one-time, half-hour show.

To say that it was not a success is an exaggeration. Bob was upset about it. He did not like television. He was reluctant to work on television, simply because he'd never done it. He was a radio guy. In fact, he talked with the producer of his radio show and asked, "Why wasn't it funny?" I thought that was lovely.

The WGN program department asked me to do another show with Bob. They said, "You have to understand, it won't be the kind of show you had last time." Well, thank God.

I told them you couldn't give Bob a lot of written material. He's a tremendous talker. I heard him doing something on the radio show one time: Bob Collins explains baseball. That's what I wanted to do for this new show. We put this thing together and did a piece about the old Wrigley Field. We went down to Rush Presbyterian hospital, near Cook County hospital. That's where the Cubs used to play. We got a lady from the area who talked about the old days, we got some good pictures, and she gave us some good information.

Southpaws are called that because in that old ballpark, as they do in Comiskey Park, the pitchers would pitch toward the northwest, which put their left arms on the south side.

She talked about the expression, "You're out in left field." That came about because near left field was a mental hospital where patients used to hang out the windows and watch the games.

We did some other pieces, including an interview with Mike Pyle, the former center for the Bears. Very good guy. He'd retired and was talking about playing football in Wrigley Field. Everyone and their dog has now forgotten that's where the Bears used to play football.

The funniest 16 or 17 minutes ever on television was what Bob did next. Strictly ad lib. Got three ballplayers, Jody Davis, Rick Sutcliffe, and a third player. Rick threw pitches and we let Bob bat. Hilarious. The comments of the players and Bob were just tremendous. I was going to cut this segment to about five minutes, but I let the entire thing run; it was that good.

That's the kind of stuff Bob did best.

We did one more special. Something about Winterfest, which included a piece about ice sculpture and another on motorcycling on ice. Well, Bob was scared to death. I can remember him sitting on that motorcycle, riding on the ice, and he had big saucer eyes.

He loved cars and owned about seven million of them. So he liked to go around and gawk at cars. We had him interviewing people at the Auto Show, down at McCormick Place. He'd come in Saturday morning and we'd tape a bit.

We used to do a piece with a guy named Mark Sweet, a magician, and he worked in the automobile display. Anyway, Mark would do these things that would confound Bob.

One time they were going to do a bit where they were going to cut Bob in half. They tried to put the device around Bob, but with his ample girth, they couldn't get it around. It would have taken two of them. Lots of good laughs.

We got in the middle of the third show and there was a cost-cutting move. They decided not to have any more of these specials. Bob was very upset. We had done some things that he wanted to get on the air, but he had more things he would have done.

I don't think Bob was a great television entertainer, but what he did so well on radio, which was talk, he did well on television. He listened to people, responded to them, had a great sense of humor.

As a *Daily Herald* Columnist, Bob Didn't Avoid Tough Issues

Colin O'Donnell

Colin O'Donnell is deputy managing editor at the Daily Herald *in Arlington Heights, Illinois.*

My boss and I had kicked around some names in November 1997 of people we wanted to pursue to see if they would write a column for us. They had to be well-known and have a Chicago feel, because they would be on the Chicago page. The first one we wanted to try was Bob.

I called Bob's office and left a message with his secretary. A day or two later, Bob tried to reach me in the morning at work to come on the show and talk about it. Luckily, I wasn't in yet. I called him back later and we chatted, and I agreed to talk with him on his show the following day. I got a glimpse of the family feel in his office when his secretary told me they were all so happy that I asked him to do this. They were so excited for him.

He was very interested and excited about doing it. He surprised his bosses at the *Chicago Tribune* though, when he had me on the radio live to talk about it. They weren't happy. And they tried to scuttle the whole thing over the next couple months. But Bob was insistent about doing it. His answer to them about why us, rather than the *Tribune:* They asked me.

Anyway, Bob went on vacation after Christmas and while in Arizona pumped out about seven or eight sample columns. To my surprise, they, for the most part, were very well done. Interesting, down to earth, concise columns about topics he was interested in. He was concerned about coming up with ideas at first, but I think he found that was easy—he had so many things happening in his life and on the radio show that, I think, it was more a question of which ones to write about.

His columns, which began in February 1998, were a complete success in my view. He attracted his loyal listeners plus, I think, he attracted nonlisteners. Just like on the radio, he had an engaging style that people liked for the most part. There are the few grammarians who took issue with some of his down-home words, but those were few. In the beginning he was worried because he wasn't getting a lot of feedback from readers. But that changed and picked up quite a bit.

In the beginning, Bob was worried that he wouldn't know how to write and looked forward to being edited. As it went on, he was more protective of how he wrote and what he said, but he was never hard to work with. We let him do what he wanted for the most part. And for the most part, I was happy with the topics he chose and how he wrote them.

He always kept his column length in check and his ideas were clear. He touched on things that everyone deals with; that's why he connected with people. Sometimes he'd stray into politics—he's unabashedly conservative and is friends with most of the high-level Republicans in the state, including Gov. Ryan. But even then, what he had to say was important. His last column was about how he would have handled the driver's-license scandal differently if he were advising the governor. Other columns also told of his uncertainty over time that the death penalty was warranted, and his views on gun control and other hot topics.

I always enjoyed talking with Bob. The easiest way to get him was by cell phone, because he was always on the move. We met a few times for lunch, and he was always interested in how I was doing; how work was; getting to know me a little bit. We had a nice lunch just after he decided to sign a new contract with WGN. He also decided he would keep writing the column. Sure, he wanted more money (who doesn't?) but that wasn't what motivated him to write the column. He liked that it gave him a chance to fully explain himself on issues and topics, and he liked that we allowed him to do that with little interference. It was a nice partnership, and I miss dealing with him.

Chapter 5

• • • • • • •

Chicago Personalities
and Friends

Bob Collins emceed Barbara Richardson's 70th birthday celebration.

You Have to Be Proud of Him

Barbara Richardson

Barbara Richardson is the coroner of Lake County, Illinois.

Shortly after I became coroner, I got to know Bob. He and my predecessor, Mickey Babcox, were friends. Bob would come to fund-raisers for Mickey. He was very involved with Fred Foreman and other politicians in Lake County. We were at events together.

I asked him if he would come to my fund-raisers, and even though he didn't know me that well, he always agreed. Most recently, he was the emcee at a party to celebrate my 70th birthday. Actually, he was in Springfield that day, and he drove back in a hurry to be at that party.

The most precious photographs I have are those taken of him at that time.

To me, that event summed up the kind of man he was. I am a nobody, and he drove from Springfield to come to my 70th birthday party. People were so thrilled to see him. He had such a following. I consider him such a dear friend. He was so supportive.

I always woke up with him. I'd have him on in the car. When he was done, I'd turn the radio off.

Bob often talked with me on the air. After he'd mention my name in the morning, I would be bombarded with people saying, "I heard you on Bob Collins." It meant a lot to me. What he said, they believed. He helped my credibility.

His line would be, "This is Barbara Richardson. She makes house calls."

Well, Bob's death was one house call I didn't want to make. I've been in office 23 years, and I still have nightmares about Bob's accident. I can't get it out of my head.

He tried very hard to steer that plane away from people and he did a good job of it, even though it took his life and the life of his friend. You have to be so proud of him for that. Thank God he didn't hit a school or something. He was trying so hard not to hit that hospital.

He was such a big teddy bear. I share in his Salvation Army charity. We were having a big kickoff one year. Someone suggested that I call Bob Collins, and he said yes immediately. We had the biggest crowd we ever had. Everyone wanted to see Bob Collins. He never denied someone anything if he could possibly provide it.

We had such fun with him. He joked about things. He got away with joking about things because it was always in good taste.

That's a rare, rare commodity. He made people feel good about themselves.

A Friend of Both Republicans and Democrats

Lee Daniels

Rep. Lee Daniels was a good friend of Bob Collins'. These sentiments were included in a resolution cosponsored by Daniels, which was approved by the Illinois House of Representatives.

Bob Collins grew up in Florida, attended the University of Florida, and started his job at WGN radio in Chicago in 1974. He quickly became one of America's premier radio personalities, who entertained and informed millions of listeners around the midwest with his sense of humor and good-natured common sense. With deep affection he was known to the public as "Uncle Bobby" due to his good and kind-hearted nature.

He was never afraid to poke fun at himself or at those who took themselves too seriously. His presence in our homes every morning was a gentle and welcome respite from life's daily challenges.

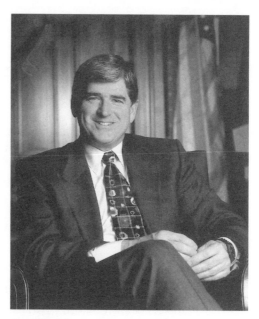

Bob Collins had many elected officials who were his friends, and although he was a strong conservative, his friendships included both Republicans and Democrats.

He was fortunate to be married since June of 1986 to Christine Collins, a native of Elmhurst, Illinois, who

Lee Daniels

was his constant companion and usually accompanied him on his many adventures and quests.

Bob Collins' love of life, Christine, and his career was evident and helped to make him a joyful and welcome part of the nation's broadcasting scene.

He was an unabashed believer in the good that is within all of us. And while he traveled extensively, he loved America, loved Illinois, loved Chicago, and felt his job at WGN was the best one in the world.

Bob Collins loved life, fast cars, fast planes, and his beloved Harley-Davidson motorcycles. He was renowned for his generosity of time, effort, and spirit in countless charitable causes; he often quietly and without fanfare helped friends and colleagues behind the scenes simply because he was a man of enormous loyalty and generosity.

Bob Collins' death will be mourned by millions throughout the nation. We mourn, along with all who knew and loved him, the death of Bob Collins as a celebrity, as a man, as a broadcaster, as a husband, as an enthusiast of life, and as an American.

Fair Questions without Sucker Punches

James R. Thompson

James R. Thompson holds the record as the longest-serving governor in Illinois, from 1977 to 1991. He is now chair of the law firm Winston & Strawn in Chicago.

I was on Bob's show many times, often on the spur of the moment. I'd call him up, especially if I was out campaigning. This got to be a ritual.

One of my favorite campaign spots in the whole state is the Jefferson Park El stop in Chicago. You get people from four or five city wards and three or four suburban townships funneling through there in a steady stream. I'd stand at the choke point and do what I call the windmill handshake as people went streaming by. You'd see

Roy Stanek

(Left to right) Former Gov. William G. Stratton, Ray Meyer, Bob Collins, and former Gov. James R. Thompson

maybe a thousand, maybe more people that morning. Very exciting, very high energy. Very early in the morning. People would get a kick that you were willing to stand there and shake hands. It was one of my favorite campaign ways to start the day.

Then I'd go to the pay phone there in the CTA station and call Bob and tell him what I was doing. He understood that was an important campaign event because you saw so many different people, you saw a whole bunch of swing voters.

He was such a gracious host. He was one of those rare individuals who could convey a smile or a laugh in his voice. If he wasn't agreeing with you on something, he wouldn't say so. He wouldn't confront you, but the tone of his voice would just change slightly.

It reminded me in a way of Floyd Kalber. When Floyd was doing the nightly newscast, he'd deliver the news straight. But if he disagreed with something that somebody said on the newscast or from a clip, a public official or someone like that, he would just so slightly raise his eyebrows. If you were a regular Floyd Kalber viewer, you knew exactly what he was saying. That was one of the most devastating things he could do.

Bob had that same sort of trick in his voice. His voice would change just a little bit. If you listened to him on the radio, and he was talking to somebody and you knew he wasn't quite agreeing with him but he didn't want to say so, his voice would change a little bit.

He did amazing things with his voice. It was part of his way to reach out to millions of fans that he had. When you think about it, that's a very powerful thing. In this age of television, in this age of show-business personality, to be able to communicate so effectively and so widely and so lovingly with just your voice is an amazing thing.

He was different when it came to his interview style. Different from the shock jocks and the guys who chase you down the street. He was in a class by himself when it came to showing respect for the office. In these days it's fashionable to bash politics, bash politicians, and it's never-ending, especially with the advent of cable television and local news competition. Chicago is probably the top news-competition town in the United States. There's no place where it's fiercer than here.

People's respect for public office gets trampled sometimes in that rush. Bob never did that. He wouldn't fawn over people; he'd ask the questions that needed to be asked. But he was a good listener; he'd let you make your point, never cut you off. He treated everybody on his show with respect whether he agreed with them or not. That's a rare commodity. People liked doing the show for that reason.

He let you talk. You were his guest and he treated you as a guest, not as a subject. And yet he had his fingers on the pulse of this community, so he knew instinctively the questions to ask. All of his questions, I thought, were fair and to the point. There were no sucker punches, never any surprises. He didn't ask a question for the sake of trying to trap somebody. He asked a question for the sake of his listeners.

We used to see each other regularly at Republican events. Everybody knew he was a Republican. Everybody knew he was passionately devoted to people in public office he admired and respected. He got a great kick out of participating in presidential campaigns. We'd see each other when the president was coming into town, or when the candidate for president was coming into town. We'd see each other at the rallies and we shared that moment. That was very nice.

He had access. Politics in Chicago is a very informal business. It depends on people liking and trusting and respecting each other. And it goes across party lines.

His legacy is this: Bob set a mark in Chicago broadcasting and in Chicago human relations that will almost be impossible to reach. It's because he was so unique.

I hope his loss is not permanent. He put a smile into Chicago every morning, and that's a hard thing to achieve. You've got millions of people out there. A lot of them have difficulties and problems and challenges, and yet every one of them listened to him and thought, "Well, at least I've got one friend." I hope that's not lost. If people remember his spirit and resolve to be a little more like him, in that respect, in their dealings with other people, then it won't be lost. There will be a legacy.

Bob's Influence Spanned the Midwest

Jim Edgar

Jim Edgar is a former governor of Illinois, having served from 1991 to 1999. He is now a distinguished fellow at the University of Illinois at Urbana-Champaign.

Bob emceed a lot of my events. Over the 18 years I was secretary of state and governor, he was there. He'd jump in a plane or in a car and be there to do the event. He was a great friend.

When I first went on his program in June of 1981, I didn't know who Bob Collins was. I didn't want to go on because it was

Bill Wiegand/University of Illinois

Brenda and Jim Edgar

talk radio, and I wondered, "Who listens to talk radio? I like music."

I had started the campaign against drunk driving. So I went on Bob's program to talk about that. I thought he had a nice program and I didn't think much about it after I left. I walked out of there at about 4 p.m. and had to fly to the Quad Cities for a Republican function that night. I got to the function and a bunch of people came up to me and said they didn't think I'd make it there because they heard me on Bob Collins.

The next day I was in Peoria. The same thing happened. People came up to me and said they'd been listening to Bob Collins and heard about the drunk-driving program.

By the end of the week, I was in Marshall, which is in south-central Illinois. A friend of mine, who is a dentist, said he heard me on the Bob Collins show. I said, "You get Bob Collins all the way down here?" He said he had it on the radio every afternoon.

It dawned on me that this guy has a phenomenal reach. I told my staff that anytime they wanted me to go on Bob's show, I would do it. I was on maybe 100 times, especially that first year, when we were trying to get the drunk-driving legislation passed.

You know, a lot of people tried to block that legislation at first. One legislator (I won't say who this is) tried to block the legislation and finally decided to support it because he got tired of hearing his name on the Bob Collins show.

Bob and I became good friends. I was not only on his show a lot, but we developed a good personal relationship. Brenda and I never had time to socialize a lot, but one of the few couples we went out with were Bob and Christine. And I tell you, he was just as real off the air as he was on.

That's the other thing I want to say. For all his fame and fortune, he was a very down-to-earth person. He was so real.

He was a member of a million families throughout the Midwest. I don't know how many people came up to me after he was killed and expressed their sorrow. It was clear they had lost a member of their family.

They started their days with him. What I found refreshing is that he never tried to force his point of view on anybody. He was an honest broker of information. His listeners felt comfortable with Bob.

Of all the people I've known who have died, I had never seen the kind of grieving that was going on and still goes on throughout the Midwest for Bob Collins.

It's hard to pick one memory that I'll remember the most, but I do have a funny story I think of often. We have our grandson, Dakota. Well, there are millions of people who think his name is Coyote, because that's what Bob always called him. I took him to the station one day when Dakota was about five months old. I had to laugh because Bob didn't have a clue what to do with this baby. For the first time, he was speechless.

A Fair and Professional Journalist

Richard Daley

Richard Daley is mayor of Chicago.

Bob Collins was much more than an outstanding radio personality. He was a very fair and professional journalist as well.

I was on his show many times, and I was always impressed by how well prepared he was. He knew how to ask tough questions without belittling the person he was interviewing. His goal was always to inform his listeners, rather than to draw attention to himself.

Friend, Supporter, Lunch Companion

Gary DelRe

Gary DelRe is the sheriff of Lake County, Illinois.

Despite of the fact that he was a large man, Bob was very gentle. He understood better than others the enormous job that law enforcement is confronted with each and every day. He had a spot of kindness in his heart for the role of police officers.

I met him through Lake County Judge Christopher Stark. Now that's a funny story, too. Chris Stark was listening to Bob's broadcast one day when Bob was commenting on the legal aspect of something. Chris called in and said, "Bob you're wrong. That's not what that law means."

Bob asked if Chris would be his official judge and legal spokesman. As a result of that, they became good friends. They socialized with their wives.

Judge Stark introduced me to Bob when we were going on a boat ride.

I invited Bob for lunch on one of the police boats. I can tell you he enjoyed eating lunch.

Bob emceed my fundraisers. Everybody who met him felt how warm he was. He made instant friendships.

Because he was a radio personality and not a television one, people didn't always recognize Bob. So if you went out to a restaurant with him, it might take a while for someone to figure out who this man was. Once he started to talk, though, someone would recognize that unique voice of his. He would stop lunch and be as gracious as he could be.

He was a very dear person. I don't know anyone who didn't like him. I was certainly very fond of him.

I had the misfortune to visit the crash site. That was a painful experience.

I was convinced that morning as I was driving to the crash site from my home in Mundelein that it was Bob in that plane. I had already been given information from my officers.

AP/Wide World Photos

The tragic aftermath of the midair accident that took Bob Collins' life.

I've been in law enforcement nearly 30 years. That's one of the most painful experiences I've had in some time.

There's been speculation about the last transmission from his plane. I don't know if that's been verified as Bob's voice or not. I don't think he had a great deal of time to react. I think a man of his composure would have tried to regain control of that plane. Just having visited that crash scene, it was nothing short of a stroke of magic that more people weren't seriously injured or killed. The other plane landed practically in the middle of a street. Bob's plane entered the fifth floor of a hospital. They had just concluded a meeting moments before. It was an eerie scene.

An Instant Friend

Dick Duchossois

Dick Duchossois is president of Arlington International.

I don't remember how or when I met Bob Collins. He would come out to the racetrack, and I just got to know him. When you meet Bob, you feel you've known him all your life. He's that type of personality. It's difficult to remember when you first met him because at that first meeting, you feel you've known him all of your life.

He spoke as a master of ceremony at Gov. George Ryan's inauguration. He had things prepared and he came across so naturally, just like he was doing it every day. But before he went out there, he was shaking like a high-school kid going on stage his first time. He was so human like the rest of us.

He had the tremendous ability to speak. Every time he opened his mouth to say something about somebody, good words came out. The thing that differentiates Bob from many in the media is this: Many people think it's stylish to criticize. Bob was so popular because he praised. He saw the good in people and didn't look at the bad. Regardless of how bad somebody was, he would find something good about them.

I had Bob out on my boat, which he loved. What I noticed was that he was the same every place you saw him. He had the same personality. So many people, especially in the media, have two personalities: one they use while working and the other when they're out of the public eye. Bob had one personality, a wonderful, friendly one. If he was interviewing you on the radio, or if he was sitting in your living room, he'd ask the same kinds of questions. He was always trying to draw people out.

People just took to him, which is where that "Uncle Bobby" developed.

He was the kind of guy who liked to have fun. I never saw him gamble much, though. He would place two dollars on a horse, that's about it. I never saw him just come out to the track to gamble; he wasn't that kind of guy. He came out for social functions, and while he was here, he was automatically part of every crowd.

He was an easygoing, lovable type of guy. You just wanted to be with him. He could talk on any subject. Any subject you brought up, he was knowledgeable about it. He must have done a tremendous amount of reading. He could talk on politics, baseball, football, and business, most anything. He really loved WGN and the people down there.

He was not a formal-type guy. I think the most uncomfortable I ever saw him was when he had to wear a tux. I saw him in Springfield wearing a tux. He was good friends with George Ryan. I think they were so close because they are so much alike. The governor is an easygoing guy. When you sit down and visit with the governor, you think you grew up together from boyhood. It was the same way with Bob. The two of them would joke back and forth. It was always in a nice way. I don't think I ever heard either of them tell an off-color story, just good stories.

Bob could be happy about just about anything. He always had a twinkle in his eye. It wasn't a teasing twinkle, more of a sparkle. Life was happy. Everything about Bob was happy. I never saw him depressed. He was contagious. It was almost like the measles. If he was laughing, you were laughing with him. If he was dead serious, you were dead serious. You just follow what he was doing in a natural way. He was a leader, a very strong leader, in a very subtle way.

He never dominated a conversation, but he controlled it. That's very important. He could sell anything he wanted to sell. And because of his integrity and honesty, people never questioned him. If he said it was good, it was good.

In a Class by Himself

Lee Rodgers

Lee Rodgers was on WIND in Chicago when it was the most popular radio station in America in the 1960s. He has been a talk-show host with ABC in San Francisco for the past 16 years.

Although we never worked together, Bob and I shared two mutual enthusiasms: flying and radio.

It's perhaps revealing that my last communication with him had to do with our continued enthusiasm for radio. We'd long since passed the point of working out of financial necessity.

Bob spoke longingly and wistfully of his plans to make his home on Pinnacle Peak in Scottsdale, where he might pursue his love of flying in the clear Arizona skies as well as exploring the mountains by motorcycle.

We were both facing career and life decisions. Our contracts ended at about the same time, and we wondered whether to renew or pursue a more leisurely life that didn't

Lee Rodgers

call for rising in the middle of the night to go "make magic" on the radio.

We resolved it the same way. And for the same reason. Because we didn't have the answer to the question, "What happens when I wake up some morning and say, 'What now?'" Why would he walk away from a job he loved to do?

My first thought when word of Bob's death hit the screen in my cabin onboard a cruise ship off the coast of South America was, "Oh, Bobby…if only…." I dismissed it with the admittedly weak consolation that his life ended doing something he truly loved, and he was still pursuing the career in which his native likability and unpretentiousness had made him such a success.

I always thought that Bob's success as a broadcaster was a direct result of not sounding like a broadcaster. Rather, more like the guy you always hoped your new next-door neighbor would be.

The term "personality" is liberally applied to broadcasters who are given any sort of leeway to express themselves on the air. Sometimes that personality is real, often it isn't. In Bob's case, neither listeners nor broadcasting colleagues ever had to doubt. If he wasn't in a class by himself, he was in a very, very small one.

The Best Relationship Person in the World

Corky Peterson

Corky Peterson is a friend of the Collins family. This is taken from the eulogy he delivered at Bob Collins' funeral.

In life, I believe, we categorize people, we put them in pews, we find a place for everybody. We talk about someone as being the greatest president ever; she was perhaps the most wonderful tennis star to ever play the game; or he was perhaps the greatest boxer in history. We'll never see one like him.

So where do we put Bob? What category do we put Bob in?

I think it's easy. I think I know exactly where Bob goes. Bob was absolutely the greatest relationship person in the whole world.

AP/Wide World Photos

Christine Collins embraces Dan Bitton, after his reading of a prayer at Bob Collins' funeral.

That's it. Bob had a reasonably good voice for the radio. His laugh was absolutely contagious. And he could engage most anybody in a really interesting conversation. Above all else, Bob knew better than anybody in the whole world how to hold a relationship. He knew how to be a son. He knew how to be an uncle. He knew how to be a brother. And he knew how to be a friend. And, certainly, he knew how to be a very loving husband.

How many times were you listening to the radio when he called down to Florida, talked to Jack and Candy, and at the end of the conversation he'd say, "Dad, I love ya, and make sure you tell Mom I love her, too"?

Or as recently as Tuesday morning (the day he died), Bob read a list of "What I Learned at Different Times in My Age." When he finished that, Christine happened to be listening and heard it. She sent Bob an e-mail. She said, "Bob, I love you."

That was at 8:30.

At 8:32, Bob responded back via e-mail to Christine. "I love you."

Bob knew what was required to have a relationship.

Think about it. Didn't we all feel bound to him? Didn't we get up every morning listening to him? We brushed our teeth with him. We had coffee with him. We drove to work, angered about the traffic, but every day Bob was there. And, you know, he made us giggle; sometimes he made us laugh out loud.

But I don't think a morning went by when you didn't at least smile a little bit at something that Bob said.

He had a great gift of making everyone within earshot feel like they were close to him, like they were a friend.

I don't think Bob was a character as much as he had character. I think he had more character than anyone else I ever met. His character was honesty. His character was moral integrity.

Those of us who were close to him had a chance to know him away from the radio station will tell you that everything he ever said on the radio, every opinion he ever expressed, any feeling he had, those were real. Those were Bob and 24 hours a day, that's what Bob was feeling.

He was never anyone but Bob. He was honest. He was God-fearing. He knew how better to be a man and how better to carry on a relationship than anybody.

Christine used to call him "that big, lovable galoot." And he was. He just was a guy who wasn't afraid to cry with you. He wasn't afraid to come up and hug you any time at all. He really knew how to express his feelings, and he knew how to make you feel close.

Bob loved that. He lived for that. That was his life. That's what he did.

That was the best part of Bob. He knew who he was. He was his own man. He never put on airs. He never let anybody think anything other than that's who he was. Whether he was in a T-shirt or in a tie, you knew who Bob was 24 hours a day.

I'd like to tell you one quick story. More than 20 years ago when Bob was early on in his career, he was doing a talk show. I don't know the why of it, but he took an interest in emergency-medical procedures. He probably read something in a story about something that it was done to save someone.

In any event, he asked his producer, "Couldn't you get me an emergency-medical person that could perhaps come on the show and I could talk to them, I could interview them." So his producer arranged that.

The following day Bob interviewed an emergency-medical person. They talked about how you help someone who's choking, how you resuscitate somebody with mouth-to-mouth resuscitation, which I'm certain there were plenty of jibes and laughs about.

About a week later, Bob got a letter from a young mother who was writing Bob to tell him how grateful she was for that show. It seemed that during her work that day she had listened to the show, paid a little bit of attention to him, picked up some high-lights.

The following day she came into her daughter's room, and her daughter had tried to swallow a toy and was choking. The woman was able to free the toy and resuscitate the child, and, of course, the child lived.

That letter has been framed and in Bob's possession for a long, long time. It's currently in his office on the wall. Over these many years of a very successful career, Bob collected awards, commen-dations, and umpteen praises. I will tell you that letter is without question Bob's most valued possession.

He knows and he felt that it was something, a little some-thing, that he was involved in that helped to do something for some-one else, that made that person's life better. And he is so awfully proud of that. It was the most important thing for Bob and that's why he treasured it so much.

I think that's the summation of Bob. He wanted to help every-body else. He couldn't do enough for you.

He was my friend. He was our friend. He was my big brother. And we're going to love him. We miss him.

Getting "Hongri" with Bob

Barry Golin

Barry Golin lives in Chicago. A pharmacist, he is president of Barry's Drugs, a chain of community pharmacies. He has also been a commodity trader, stockbroker, and real-estate developer.

We first met Bob and Chris sometime in the late 1970s when he bought a house in Deerfield. My wife then (we're now divorced 10 years) used to socialize and train her Dobermans at various locations, including the Deerfield Commons shopping center. A pretty young woman introduced herself and asked if my wife trained professionally (which she did), and would she consider training her and her boyfriend's dog?

That was the beginning. The two women became friends, and soon thereafter, Chris and Bob Collins came to our house.

After a while, Bob said rather sheepishly that for some reason he thought my wife was a poor immigrant girl who trained dogs to help support her family. He now thought that was rather funny since our house was obviously custom built, three times larger than his, and a whole lot nicer. I had to explain that we were still nice, even though we weren't poor. We had a lot of laughs about that over the years. It wasn't too long before his house was twice the size of ours.

Aside from both of us having a strange sense of humor, we shared a great love of food. We became fast friends and would go out together (just Bob and me) most Saturday and Sunday mornings (about 6 or 6:30 a.m.) for breakfast. One of us would call, and the following greeting ensued: "Hongri-Hongri-Hongri!" to which the other replied where and when (usually the Smokehouse at Gilmer Road and Route 83, where the owner, Bea, knew us and we weren't embarrassed to order prodigious quantities of food).

For all the ensuing years, most of the time our phone greetings or voice messages were just the words "Hongri-Hongri-Hongri!"

In 1989 I signed on to sail from Kauai to Victoria, B.C. (about 2,600 miles across the Pacific, on a tall ship), to fulfill one of my lifelong dreams, and I had many discussions with Bob about the trip. Finally I told him that it was going to be a great adventure, and that he should get WGN-TV to assign a film crew to the voyage.

Bob, who had been sailing with me on my boat, looked at me like I was crazy.

I was envisioning fame, and some fortune, from this adventure. Bob finally said that he thought it was going to be boring for the average person, and if I wanted a film record, I should get a video camera of my own. My feelings were hurt, as I had convinced myself that this would make a great documentary.

Was he ever right; even I was bored! So the rest of that year I had to eat crow.

While Bob was doing the afternoon show shortly after he moved to Deerfield, we got a frantic call from Chris late one afternoon that the house was flooding and sinking fast. Three of us rushed over and started hauling all the living-room furniture out to the garage, as the living-room ceiling was gushing water. It turned out Bob had hired a friend of his to put in a wet bar in the entrance hall, and the only place he could run the water line was through the living-room ceiling.

Bob showed up at about 6:30, said hello, and asked Chris if the flood meant that dinner would be late.

Once we took a vacation to Aruba, and people on the plane heard his voice and kept asking if he was Bob Collins. He would point at me, and say I was Bob Collins. Even in the gambling casino at 3 a.m., people would recognize his voice and come up to pay a compliment.

Once at Lou Mitchell's, the waitress asked how Bob wanted his toast, and he replied, "Brown."

When Bob and Chris were getting married in Las Vegas, he wanted her to ride out with him on his motorcycle, to which she replied: "You ride; my mother and I are flying."

We talked on the phone two weeks before that fatal flight and were lamenting how long it had been since we'd seen each other. We made plans to get together the following month for dinner with our wives. There is hardly a day that goes by that I don't miss him. He was truly my good friend.

Bob Was a Lot Like Harry Caray

Dutchie Caray

Dutchie Caray is one of Chicago's great ladies and the widow of Harry Caray.

Steve Green

Dutchie and Harry Caray

Harry knew Bob through WGN, passing him in the hallways, going to different affairs. Bob would call and ask Harry about things he talked about on the air. He used Harry as a resource. We saw each other at Tribune Company functions.

Bob Collins reminded me a lot of Harry. They were both celebrities in this city, but talking to them, you'd never know it. Harry was probably a bigger celebrity than Bob, but he never thought he was any better than anyone else, or tried to put on airs. Bob was the same way. What you saw is what you got. He didn't try to be like somebody else.

You know movie stars and people like that who put on airs or try to be something bigger than they are. Bob wasn't that way at all.

Whenever Harry saw Bob, he would call out, "Uncle Bobby!" That's how he would greet him. "Look, Uncle Bobby in person!"

A Neighbor Remembers Bob

Bill Dunn

Bill Dunn lives in Libertyville, Illinois.

February 8, 2000, was a day like the many thousands of days I woke up to the voice, cackle, and laugh of Bob Collins. I didn't know that it was going to change.

I miss Bob Collins in many ways. Not only did I wake up with Bob, but I read his weekly column in the local paper. I even liked knowing that he lived just over the tracks from the forest preserve where I biked in the morning.

Bob Collins and I shared the distinction of starting new jobs on March 10, 1986. That morning he took over the morning slot from Wally Phillips, and I started my new career at Baxter Healthcare Corporation. I can still recall the feeling as I looked into the mirror and straightened my tie.

I saw my face but heard Bob's voice. As I drove to work, I felt that he and I "sort of" worked together. I could easily relate as he shared the awkward experiences of starting a new job. Filling the big shoes left by "Wally who?" new people, faces, bosses, rules, "Memo Fairies," dress codes, cafeteria food, etc. were all parts of the same scary new world that I was experiencing, but we faced it together.

Bob's dialogue with the public, banter with the studio staff, sophomoric humor, quips, and barbs entertained me. As he settled in, I could see and feel other facets of Bob's wonderful personality. He could really get "engaged" in a subject and let you know where he stood. He had a fuse, sometimes long, sometimes short. On a number of occasions he even yanked my chain. But then, that was Bob. His love and affection for his parents was especially heart-warming. He loved people, and people loved him.

I was six months younger than Bob. I shared his liking for moon pies, biscuits and gravy, grits, and cracklins. His anecdotes about his school days spawned familiar memories. I even related to his hometown of Lakeland, Florida. Almost 20 years ago, I had the opportunity to take my wife and five daughters to Florida for the very first time. I had to deliver, install, and demonstrate a grocery-store checkout counter I designed for Publix Foods in Lakeland. After the demo we went to Disney World. I'll always remember the trip to Lakeland and Disney World.

Bob Collins needed and protected his "space." Bob lived a little ways from our village. One summer he was the grand marshal in our "Libertyville Days" parade. I was never introduced to Bob socially, but I "bumped" into him at a health club and introduced myself. I would see him occasionally around town and say, "Hey Bob," smile, and give him the "thumbs up." He would look over, grin, and return the gesture. Although it would have been easy for me to close the social space, I didn't. I believe that he knew I respected his space and appreciated my judgment. A smile from Bob Collins was worth it.

Speaking of health and exercise, one spring day I left the office early to do some yardwork at home. About three blocks from home, whom do I see peddling toward me on the road? None other than Bob Collins. He was laboriously cranking on an old balloon-tire bike as he zigged and zagged up the road on his way home. As I approached him, I slowed down, stuck my head out of the window, and said, "Now there's a sight." Bob looked up and shouted back, "Yeah, and it's killing me." We both laughed and went on our ways. On another occasion, I was mowing our lawn on my old (1965) John Deere lawn tractor. Bob was out on a Gull Wing that he had just gotten. As he went past me, I waved; he shouted, "Nice tractor," and I shouted, "Nice bike."

One week before Bob's death, I was riding Amtrak's "Southwest Chief" back to Chicago from a Creativity Conference in San Diego. I finally had time to read *Anam Cara,* a book of Celtic wisdom by John O'Donohue. In that book, a number of concepts regarding time and space are discussed. One such notion really moved me: "The only difference between us and the dead is that they are now in invisible form. You cannot see them with the human eye. But you can sense the presence of those you love and have died. With the refinement of your soul, you can sense them. You feel that they are near."

I immediately believed in that notion as a truth and the reason I feel so close to my deceased parents, relatives, and little grandson Nicholas.

I miss Bob Collins, but now I hear that voice, cackle, and laugh. As I mow the front yard and look down the street I hear him shout "Nice tractor," as I shout back, "Nice bike."

"Thumbs up," Bob.

Millions Thought He Was Their Best Friend

Jack Sayer

Jack Sayer lives in Newport Beach, California, and is an automotive consultant. He was president of Z. Frank Automotive Group (including Z. Frank Chevrolet) for 20 years.

(L. to R.) Linda Sayer, Chris Collins, Bob Collins, and Jack Sayer

I was in Chicago for surgery in the middle of January and saw Bob for lunch.

About 10 years ago my wife Linda had double-mastectomy surgery as a result of breast cancer. As you would expect, Bob was extremely upset. About that time he was doing a segment on-air about a man who lost his penis in a lawnmower accident.

Bob asked his audience if there was anything comparable that could happen to a woman. Immediately a woman called in to say the loss of a breast could be equally devastating to a woman.

At that point Bob started to reflect upon what my wife had gone through (without mentioning her by name). He talked about her courage and upbeat attitude throughout the ordeal.

The station was deluged with calls for the next few days with people telling how inspired they were by the broadcast. I have a tape of the segment.

On a more upbeat note, we invited Bob and Chris to our home for one of the Jewish Holidays. Bob asked if this was the one where we slaughtered the lamb! If so, he was concerned how Chris would react to all the blood. I told him the most exotic things he could look forward to were honey and apples!

On another occasion my wife invited them to our home for a surprise birthday party for me. He asked what the dress was, and she told him "causally elegant." He asked nothing more. He and Chris showed up on their Harleys as the two most elegant bikers you have ever seen. Full leather all the way!

As you know, Bob was very close to former Governor Jim Edgar. Jim asked Bob to give the keynote address at his inauguration. One problem: Bob didn't own a suit! So my wife took him shopping and got him outfitted.

As public a persona as he was on the air, this is how private he was in his private life. I will never forget my first visit to his home. Instead of the traditional "welcome" mat, his said, "Go away."

This was a guy who captured a market because he was everything he seemed to be. And in my case, my best friend. Interestingly, millions of people in Chicago felt the same way, and they never met him. At our lunch in January, we made plans for him to visit us when he next came to Phoenix. He was going to bike over here.

Chapter 6

• • • • • • •

Charities

John Tondelli and Bob Collins

A Renaissance Man in His Spare Time

Richard Grozik

Richard Grozik is director of communications and public relations for the Salvation Army in Chicago.

In the mid-1980s, I was director of public relations of Ducks, Unlimited, in Long Grove, Illinois. Bob called one day and asked about our organization.

It's a wetlands-conservation group. He wanted to know who supported it. I told him a lot of duck hunters and sportsmen were involved because they wanted to perpetuate the resource and their hunting heritage.

He wanted to come out and spend time in a duck blind. I took him to a place in northern Illinois off the Des Plaines River. We watched the sun come up. I identified some ducks for him. None came close enough for me to shoot, but he enjoyed the whole experience.

It was kind of cold and windy and started to spit some rain, but he didn't complain one bit.

We talked about the natural world and how a lot of it has disappeared from this part of the country because of the population moving out here. He felt good there was this organization trying to maintain wetlands, trying to maintain our natural heritage.

This was just a personal thing he wanted to do. It wasn't attached to the radio at all. He never had me on the show or anything. We had a great morning together.

I always thought that Bob Collins had a lot of things he wanted to do, but once he threw his heart and soul into his work, including getting behind the Salvation Army and being in the spotlight all the time, his time was limited.

So this was a special day for him. He was just curious. He had heard about us. He just wanted to check it out. He had no trouble with people who hunt ducks. He didn't express any problem with that. He didn't want to hunt ducks himself. He just enjoyed the experience.

He had a lot of things going on. He was a Renaissance man in what he tried to accomplish with his life, and I think he achieved it more than he'll ever know.

He'll be missed certainly here at the Salvation Army.

We've established a new award, the Bob Collins Excellence in Media Award.

Our plan is to present it each year at the Salvation Army's annual civic luncheon, held during National Salvation Army Week in May.

It will be given to the media professional who demonstrates the personal and career characteristics of a mature journalist, and whose pursuit of excellence serves as a role model for others. This individual must also exhibit a spiritual discernment and moral intelligence that enlightens his contemporaries and edifies the people whose ministry the Salvation Army holds dear.

It's our small way of giving a tribute to a man who played such a large part in the success of the Army here in Chicago. We hope it inspires others to follow in his footsteps. I hope it does.

Spreading His Magic on Michigan Avenue

Robert Cotner

Robert Cotner is director of development for the Salvation Army in Chicago.

I knew Bob through my work with the Salvation Army, primarily when he would emcee our Tree of Lights ceremony at the Hancock Center in Chicago, which happened every Wednesday before Thanksgiving at noontime.

About four years ago he started going to visit his in-laws at Thanksgiving, so it became impossible for him to do it. But for about eight years, until 1995, he was our emcee.

Bob was a tremendous enlivening force at that event. His personality and his wonderful voice just made the day. Everybody knew him, and if they didn't recognize the way he looked, they recognized his voice.

There were other people from other stations there, too. They were doing stories for their radio stations. It was fun to see them because they all talked with Bob. It wasn't a competition. They all worked together. They all knew Bob and loved him. It was a terrific experience.

One year in particular, we had this 20-minute program. We introduced the chair of the event, talked about the Salvation Army's goal for the season, introduced the celebrities, played some special music, and at the end we had a piece of fire equipment.

A basket went up in the air and we took the colonel and chair of the campaign up into that basket. They waved a magic wand over the tree and someone below plugged the sucker in, and 82,000 lights come on. Everyone cheered!

Bob turned to me and says, "How'd you like to go up in that gondola?"

So after the ceremony was finished, the firemen took Bob and me up on a special lift. We went up and up in this thing, hanging over Michigan Avenue, vibrating. The basket was swaying in the wind. I was really scared, but Bob was thrilled. He loved to do things like that.

He was frequently at our annual civic luncheon, which is our celebration during National Salvation Army Week in May. Bob would often emcee. One year he was given the highest award, the William Booth Award, for what he had done for the Army.

He was a tremendous personality, a rare, rare being. The Army was blessed by his friendship. We do miss him.

Bozo and Bob: Working for Kids

Joey D'Auria

Joey D'Auria has been Bozo on WGN-TV since 1984.

We did the Grand March for Kids, a WGN toy drive, about 10 years ago.

The first year, we did live broadcasts from Pioneer Court next to WGN in downtown Chicago. People would bring toys to us. The second year we did it in the parking lot at WGN-TV. The third and fourth years, we did it at the Rosemont Horizon because it was such a big thing by then.

Every year we would promote it and we'd hit the main offices at the Tribune Tower. We'd stop by Bob's show and give him a little presentation, a bucket with several treats in it. I was dressed as Bozo and he'd interview me on his radio show and plug the drive.

We did this two or three times. He was very cordial and enthusiastic.

Bozo the Clown

Of course, he recognized me because I was in my clown outfit. When WGN had its combined offices at Bradley Place, I would see Bob leaving the building as I was coming in. I don't think he ever recognized me because I was just in street clothes.

Like I said, when he dealt with me as Bozo, he was always friendly and helpful.

Bob was involved in a lot of charities for kids and would plug them on his show. I heard many mentions of Toys for Tots, which is a big motorcycle charity and motorcycle enthusiasts would take part in that. I know he's plugged them on his show because he was a motorcycle enthusiast.

Memories of His Uncle-ship

Robert A. Bonesteel

Bob Bonesteel is the public-relations director of the Salvation Army in Chicago. He has been a member of that group since 1967.

A few years back, I walked over to my neighboring village to see a friend at the Lombard Lilac Parade. He had been named honorary parade marshal that year. As I wended my way through the

Roy Stanek

Bob Collins and Bob Bonesteel

parade staging area, I could see his robust, bearded figure leaning against his restored World War II military Harley. Dressed in khakis and crowned with an Australian-looking bush hat, one might think he was more appropriately dressed for going on an African safari than leading a parade.

That wasn't surprising though. No one ever accused Bob Collins of being a fashion plate, although he made interesting fashion statements. His running gag with his WGN radio audience, which was more in keeping with reality than just show-biz shtick, was that he hated to wear anything even approaching the need for a tie. What was surprising was that he, of all people, had the audacity to yell at me as he looked up and our eyes met in distant recognition. "Where'd ya get that god-awful, ugly hat," he yelled as he took note of my big orange Uncle Bobby WGN Big Time Radio Star ballcap, which I had dusted off for the occasion. The nerve! Then he and I, along with Tom Petersen, who had consented to be his sidekick for the day, chatted over whatever subjects happened to come up between friends.

As I encounter people who know I've had some association with Uncle Bobby, I've gotten the ubiquitous, "What's Bob Collins really like?" Such a question asked about actors is designed to separate fact from fancy, because actors' real personalities are shrouded in the parts they play. While Bob was not an actor, he was a consummate entertainer. Still, he was but a voice to most. Those curious about Bob seemed to be trying to confirm that the radio "friend" they adopted was in fact real and not just a "part" being acted out for their radio amusement—a reality check that their loyalty hadn't been misplaced. It always gave me great pleasure to report that anytime Bob was around people, you pretty much got off-air what he was on-air.

I don't think I could have endured the responses of disappointment, had it been otherwise. If there was anything disguised in his home-spun "laughin' and scratchin'" persona, it was the depth of his education. He always chose, as any good journalist, the simple word rather than the complex one that he was equally capable of using. He would likely wince at being labeled a "journalist," although his show was a daily journal of life and Americana.

I think those closest to him would also confirm what a veteran listener of the Bob Collins show might suspect: Bob had a personal drive to perfection that he also demanded of co-workers. But no demand was any greater than that he set for himself. So what was the magic that produced the affection of so many? Bob was simply respectful of people, not the stilted, distant kind of formality one might associate with that word, but more in the nature of the words of John Wesley, who, observing a drunkard lying in a gutter, noted, "There go I but for the grace of God." A kind of respect that recognized, "We're all in this together."

He was as comfortable with the janitor as with CEOs and heads of state. He understood the important common denominators of life that make us pretty much equal, looking for the same thing: to feel worthy and to be sought. But such seeking and making others feel worthy is an exhausting business. So there was in Bob an alter ego of privacy and shyness into which most of us who must constantly extend ourselves to others must retreat and emotionally regroup in order to maintain some sense of personal equilibrium.

That part of his life was filled with trips and toys—activities and objects with which he occupied himself, while storing up the resources to be a friend when he needed to be there for others.

He knew the worth of others or at least the "could be" worth. Bob had two reactions to people who failed to see and realize their worth: anger or sadness. Anger if there were something external that made it difficult or impossible for someone to capture his or her sense of worth or sadness when a person, of his or her own volition, would throw it away. I gained an insight into that while sitting in the studio one frosty Friday morning after Thanksgiving many years ago.

Bob used to kick off the Christmas season for WGN on that Friday with a round of holiday music and Mother Ellsworth's eggnog. Bob's long, on-air draught and imitation of choking, followed by an "ahhhh" of stomach-warming delight was actually just a sip rather than an actual chug of the mixture, traditionally provided for the occasion by one station newsman, Dave Ellsworth. Collins still had three hours of show to complete, and I don't think he really "drank" all that well, notwithstanding whatever FCC rules that might have been in place.

He might have come to that conclusion himself after he and air-time sidekick Jim Loughman finally came to their senses following a round of full participation in a Chicago St. Patty's Day parade, only to realize they had left Roy Leonard stranded on-air for several hours while they partied.

On these post-Thanksgiving Fridays, it became a 13-year tradition for Bob to have me come down to the studio and stand with a Salvation Army kettle and bell. It was his way of keeping the rules, yet breaking them, a game he very much enjoyed. The station had

Roy Stanek

Jim Loughman as Gwendolyn with Bob Collins

adopted the Neediest Kids Fund as the official station charity, so station personalities who had become identified with charitable groups as Bob had with The Salvation Army didn't have the same freedom and latitude to solicit funds openly for their favorite outside groups as they were once able to do. Bob embraced the Neediest Kids Fund wholeheartedly, not just as a good company man, but in real admiration of the good work the cause did.

But he felt conflicted about the possibility of perhaps having to abandon his long-enduring commitment to The Salvation Army. So my Friday morning appearance in front of the studio gave him an opportunity to subtly subvert the letter of the law without breaking it. I would stand outside with an Army kettle and ring the bell. But 5 a.m. wasn't exactly a high-traffic time to collect street-gotten Christmas donations. For about the first two hours of the day my only prospects for donations were some pigeons perched on the ledge above, hugging the building to keep from freezing. The real gambit was that Bob would open the mic that had been installed outside on the showcase studio window so that Michigan Avenue passersby could be interviewed from the street if the talk-

show host wanted. Bob used the mic to catch the sounds of the bell
under announcer copy and the beginning of a musical selection as a
kind of constant background reminder of the Army's presence.

From time to time, we would banter back and forth and talk
about how cold it was. And sometimes it really was. On one occasion the wind had been whipping around pretty viciously, and the
wind-chill factor was well below zero. I must have looked like I
was hurting, and probably was. (Once a person gets chilled, those
kettle stints can be torturous.) He waved at me to come into the
studio and warm up. I went into the bowels of the building and
fetched a hot cup of coffee and then made my way into the studio.
Lyle Dean was seated immediately to Bob's right shuffling papers
for the news report at the top of the hour; Annie Maxfield was

*Lyle Dean (top left), Bob Collins, and Annie Maxfield pose with Chicago
firefighters.*

Roy Stanek

positioned at floor level and was talking on the phone in hushed tones getting a traffic update. Bob gestured for me to sit down next to him on his left in the broadcast chair used by Max Armstrong, Orion Samuleson, or the sports reporter. He held up the carafe of Ellsworth's concoction, as if offering for me to imbibe. He did it with a sheepish smirk of insight, knowing that a teetotaling "Sally" would certainly have to refuse. Even though the mics were closed and it was "safe" to talk in the studio, we hadn't yet exchanged words. It was quiet except for the strains of the music Bob had called up to end the hour.

Bob was kind of in a secret place that some music took him—especially this particular Christmas piece sung by Karen Carpenter. We sat there enjoying her crystalline tone and luxurious phrasing, but finally, the completing cadence neared. Bob looked up at me and said with a slow side-to-side shake of his head, "What a waste," in reference to Carpenter's death as the result of an eating disorder. The waste was that she didn't understand her worth to herself or others.

If there is anything for which I will remember Bob, it is that he understood the worth of each person. That's why he was virtually everybody's friend. You knew he thought you were worthwhile. I think that might be why he loved and admired The Salvation Army so much. He understood that it was the goal of The Salvation Army to help people realize their ultimate worth, to do in total what another Army intoned: "be all that you can be."

I never was able to get the whole story. Bob protected it as if in a competing loyalty to others. But I have managed to piece together enough to know there was a time when Bob received some personal kindness from a Salvation Army worker or program that made him feel loved or cared for, and somehow it helped prove to him that he and others he loved were worthwhile. So I just want to say thanks, Uncle Bobby, for making me (us) feel that way, too.

Cold Hands, but a Warm Heart

Karl E. Strand

Karl E. Strand is director of special efforts for the Salvation Army in Chicago. He is a fifth generation Salvationist.

When I became special-efforts director, I spent a lot of time with Bob Bonesteel making early-morning calls to the WGN radio station.

My job is to coordinate the Christmas Kettles and Donut Day efforts and those kinds of events. Bob Collins always was big in supporting those. If not physically, then verbally, by giving us coverage on the air.

There were many cold and snowy mornings we would stand outside that WGN showcase studio and freeze while he was in there making us ring the bell.

He would be inside the showcase studio doing his show. Bob Bonesteel and I would stand outside.

If it wasn't too cold, I had my horn there. Bonesteel and I would be basically the only two people on the street at 5:30 in the morning. This was right on Michigan Avenue at the Chicago River. If my horn didn't freeze up because of the wind coming off the river, I'd play tunes for the background.

Later on in the show, when people started showing up, Bob would come out and do an interview with us. He would present a visual picture on the radio, describing us freezing outside.

Of course, I don't think it was ever freezing to Bob. I'll never forget; we'd be all bundled up for the frozen tundra it was, he'd come out in his jeans and maybe a sports jacket and do the show.

Many times he came out in short sleeves. If you were ever inside his studio when he was operating, you'd understand. Although it had heat, Bob kept it very cold inside. There was hardly a temperature change from inside that booth to the cold outside.

He liked it cold in there. Your teeth would be chattering too hard; you never asked him why he kept it so cold.

Salvationists are going to miss him a lot. There aren't too many people like him who have given that kind of time to something we so strongly believe in.

He liked the people. That wasn't unusual because that's the way he was in general. I grew up in Chicago and grew up listening to Bob Collins on the air. As long as I can remember listening to WGN, I remember listening to him.

It was always a people thing with him. He had the ability to shut down somebody who was maybe getting out of control, yet he was never doing it in a rude or crude way. I always got the idea he shut you down with love.

There were many things he disagreed with, and he was never afraid to tell you that. It was a refreshing thing, especially for a radio talk show. You usually get their own points of view that never budged, or somebody who agreed with everybody who called in. With Bob you knew what you got was what he meant. He didn't have trouble telling someone his own opinion.

Little guys from the street were treated the same as governors. One morning I remember hearing him say on the air, "I like you, governor, but you're wrong." I nearly drove off the road.

With the Salvation Army, he got to meet people he really liked and knew these people liked what they were doing. I got the impression that if you liked what you were doing, he believed in you.

Why I Support the Salvation Army

Lon Rosado

J. Alonzo (Lon) Rosado is vice president of Great Lakes Data Systems, Inc., in Encinitas, California.

On February 8, 2000, there was a mid-air collision of two small airplanes in the Chicago area. As a private pilot, I am always saddened to hear about people dying in any kind of a plane crash.

But this crash was particularly sad for me and, I think, for the Salvation Army.

Bob Collins died in that crash, and Bob was one of the biggest and best supporters and promoters of the Salvation Army who has ever trumpeted a cause over the airways. His morning drive-time radio show on broadcast giant WGN was listened to by hundreds of thousands of listeners every day. I lived in Wisconsin for 20 years, and for most of those 20 years I listened to Bob Collins on the radio.

The fact is that it was Bob Collins who first persuaded me that the Salvation Army should be on my list of charitable contributions, even if there was not another single charitable organization on the list. Fact is, the Salvation Army is the only one on my list.

Bob really did do a job on me when it comes to the Salvation Army. On November 19, 1999, when their bell-ringers first show up at the malls, I spotted one as I was leaving a grocery store in Encinitas, California. I replied to his pleading look by saying, "I will get my checkbook out of the car and write you a check." I'm sure they hear lines like that all the time from people who get in their cars and blast out of there without a second thought.

Of course, having been trained by Bob Collins, I went back to the bell ringer with my personal check, for $50. I assured him that the real donation would be mailed in December but that I couldn't walk by a Salvation Army bell-ringer and not donate something. I think he probably believed me.

As a pilot, I truly hope that Bob's life hereafter is one that includes lots of great planes to fly as a fringe benefit.

I will always remember "Dead Skunk in the Middle of the Road," and I guess he finally had that long-dreaded "Unforeseen Meeting With Management," and that is the reason he didn't show up for work this morning.

One Word and We Were Saved

Dan Bassill

Dan Bassill is one of the founders and the current president and CEO of Cabrini Connections, a grassroots not-for-profit organization in Chicago.

I'd like to tell you how Bob Collins made a difference to me and nearly 100 teens living in one of Chicago's public-housing neighborhoods.

Cabrini Connections is concerned with the large number of American children who fail to obtain the basic skills and experience that will be necessary to compete for employment in the global economy of the 21st Century.

In a small charity, CEO means "covers every option" ranging from putting stamps on letters to transporting kids to getting supplies and volunteers to strategic planning and selling the product. Our small charity believes that tutoring/mentoring programs can make a huge difference in the lives of at-risk youth. However, such programs must be well-structured, diverse, long-term, and innovative in the ways they attract volunteers, students, donors, and ideas.

I've been involved with mentoring since 1973, first as a volunteer tutor working with a 4th-grade boy named Leo. We'd meet every Tuesday after work, and I often did not know what to do or if I was doing any good. However, Leo's mom kept encouraging me to come back, saying, "He talks about you all the time." I came back a second year and served as a leader of a volunteer committee, and in the third year I became the leader of the volunteer group that organized the program. I stayed in this role until 1990, all the while building a career which by 1980 was a management position in the advertising department of Montgomery Ward, which hosted the program.

Over the years, my experience connecting children and adults in one-on-one mentoring grew, as did my passion for mentoring as a way to bring not only children and adults together, but to unite diverse groups of adults in ways in which everyone's life was enriched from the experience. My connection with Leo has lasted to this day. I've been at every one of his graduations, starting with eighth grade, then high school (Lane Tech), then college (Memphis State).

I was even a guest at his wedding, where his father greeted me "as part of the family." I know how important this association has been, to me, and to Leo.

And as a leader of a program, which by 1992 had engaged nearly 3,000 adults with 3,000 kids in long-term mentoring, I know that many other lives have been enriched in the process.

In 1990 I left Ward and converted this original program into a non-for-profit. Two years later I left this non-for-profit and formed Cabrini Connections. I left my leadership position in the original second-through-sixth-grade tutoring program in the fall of 1992 and with a few supporters created Cabrini Connections. We did this because we knew there was a need for tutor/mentor programs serving seventh-through-12th-grade teens and a need for an infrastructure, which could mentor other programs in Chicago.

We formed Cabrini Connections in the weeks following the shooting death of little Dantrel Davis. While the public and the media were shouting for more programs like ours to surround kids with love and opportunity so there would not be future shootings, I knew from 17 previous years of experience in this movement that these outcries seldom lasted, seldom reached into every neighborhood where kids lived in poverty, and that there was no systemic plan (or leadership commitment) to help existing tutor/mentor programs grow, while helping new programs fill voids.

Starting with seven volunteers, no money, and a deep commitment, we formed Cabrini Connections in 1993. By June of 1999 we had built the program to an annual enrollment of nearly 100 student participants, ranging from seventh-graders to high-school seniors.

While the organization is committed to helping each of its 100 teens move to careers, it recognized the small impact this number would have on the huge need in Chicago. Without an effort to create quality after-school tutor/mentor and school-to-career programs in every poverty neighborhood of the city and suburbs, the poor people of the region would continue to be left out of the economic opportunities and benefits the region offers, the schools would continue to struggle to educate kids who have little framework for learning, and the next generation of welfare would continue to grow.

We dedicated one-half of our efforts to building this infrastructure. We call it the Tutor/Mentor Connection, a detailed action plan aimed at sustaining and expanding the availability and quality of after-school programs throughout Chicago.

Our work has been recognized in dozens of print and media stories. Yet in the summer of 1999 we almost went out of business.

From 1993 until March 1999 a growing number Kids' Connection volunteer mentors and students met weekly at the Cabrini Connections Center on the 21st floor of the Montgomery Ward Headquarters building on Chicago Avenue.

However, while Cabrini Connections was growing from year-to-year, Ward was moving into financial difficulties that led to a change of management then a declaration of bankruptcy in 1997.

In the spring of 1999, as part of its strategy to regain profitability, Ward sold its office buildings along Chicago Avenue and concentrated its employees into the corporate tower where Cabrini Connections had been operating. In June a date was given when the agency had to vacate the building. That date was July 15, 1999.

This decision on the part of Ward was not unexpected. However, while Cabrini Connections was growing, it has never been more than one or two months' cash flow from being broke. While new donors helped expand revenue each year, many donors did not repeat from year to year. Cabrini Connections had not been able to find deep-pocketed donors to help us rent retail office space in the Cabrini-Green area, which over the past years has increased dramatically in price due to conversion of many office and warehouse buildings to condos. The organization also had not had the means to find new donors or donated space. It had a problem.

We turned to the media to get our story and call for help to the public.

I had been an off-and-on listener to the Bob Collins morning show since he came to Chicago. Merri Dee of WGN-TV has been one of the strongest supporters of Cabrini Connections and a major financial supporter.

However, I'd never met Bob.

When he heard of our need, Bob Collins invited me to appear on his show. It was quite a thrill to be sitting at the table across from Bob. He was so casual that it was comfortable for me to be there. And when he talked of my charity and our work, he was the best advocate we could have ever found. I had heard of how he could make a commercial come to life. He made our cause come to life that morning. One person who heard him that day immediately sent us a $5,000 contribution.

Thanks to Bob's efforts and the response of many others to our call, Cabrini Connections survived the 1999 move and continues to tutor and mentor kids in Cabrini-Green while helping kids in other programs also have brighter futures. We're not out of the woods, however. We still have nearly $70,000 in new annual expenses that we didn't have before the move from Ward. We're split into two different buildings separated by six blocks of Cabrini-Green. We still do not have a major benefactor who can assure long-term success. However, we would not have made it to this year if Bob had not come to our rescue. We thank him.

I was really shocked when I was driving home from work late the evening Bob died. During the following days as people talked about him, his style, his office, etc., my mind brought back the memory of sitting next to him, of hearing the banter, of seeing the doughnuts. I even went out and bought a box of doughnuts and told my co-workers these were the Bob Collins Memorial Doughnuts.

I received a call a few weeks ago from another person who had been helped by Bob when his dad was dying of cancer. This person had read the note I'd put in Bob's memorial book on the WGN website. It prompted him to call me and offer to support Cabrini Connections with his company. I was surprised, and more than pleased.

I've learned in many ways over the years that "when one door closes, another opens." We try to teach this to our kids. I've had to learn this myself.

When Bob died we lost a friend on Earth. But when this caller phoned me, I said, maybe we've gained a friend in heaven. Maybe this for us was a way for Bob to pass on his concern for us and many other charities so that many of Bob's friends would be motivated to reach out to all of the causes Bob was supporting and say, "Bob sent me."

We thank Bob Collins for taking the time to help us, as he has so many others. He will be missed, but his memory and his message will live on in the work of all of those he has influenced.

Chapter 7

•••••••

Flying and Motor-sickles

Bob Collins

His First Solo Flight: 7:20 a.m.

Vern Jobst

A retired United Airlines pilot, Vern Jobst taught Bob Collins how to fly using a Cessna 152.

Bob's first flying lesson was on December 31, 1977. I had been flying the Spirit of St. Louis replica, and Bob came out to Du

Page airport and took a ride. He was going to talk about it on the radio, which we did a lot.

He seemed to really enjoy flying, and after a while, he asked me if he could learn how to fly. I told him I could find any number of good flight instructors. "No," he said, "I want you."

Well, I was on the Lindbergh tour for another three months or so. He and I seemed to hit it off, so I told him he'd have to wait until I was available.

He took his first dual ride with me. He soloed the following spring. Anytime I solo somebody for the first time, I look at the time they took off. It's kind of like what people do when a baby is born or when they get married. You look at the time so you can record it. I looked at my watch and he took off at 7:20 in the morning. That was kind of cute. You know, WGN, 720-AM.

Bob was a great pilot. We say that if someone is a good pilot, they have good hands and feet. Bob had great hands and feet.

He talked about the fun of being up in the air. He really enjoyed it.

I consider Bob Collins my best friend. He was very close to my family. In fact, he became an uncle to my daughter Jennifer. He liked her so much, he'd drive out to visit us and ask if it was okay to take Jennifer out for a ride on his motorcycle, or out skiing. He was like that, a big kid at heart.

I'll Always Call Him Uncle Bobby

Jennifer Jobst

Jennifer Jobst is a loan officer for Bank of America in Memphis, Tennessee. She is the daughter of Vern Jobst, who taught Bob Collins how to fly.

I'll always call him Uncle Bobby. Every morning I would get up and e-mail Uncle Bobby and he would e-mail me right back.

That's been hard. I wake up in the morning and I want to get over to the computer and send him a message.

I met him when I was little. I don't even remember how old I was, but I was about seven or so. He really was like an uncle to me. He was such a big part of our family.

He would come over and take me out on his motorcycle. It was like having your best friend come over. He'd visit with my dad and then we'd take off.

We'd also go downhill skiing. Just the two of us. He really liked doing things with me. I always wanted to go out to a good restaurant, but I remember he said he wanted to go to the kinds of places where they bolted the stools to the ground.

I remember when my dog died. I was older by then. My parents were out of town and my dog was sick. I wasn't sure what to do, so I called Uncle Bobby at the radio station. And do you know what he did? He canceled his show that morning and drove to our home so he could be with me and help me with our dog. Now that's something!

Another time, my grandmother died, and I was having a really hard time with it. I remember at the funeral, Uncle Bobby put his hand on my shoulder. I just leaned on him and he walked me to the car and put me inside. He took care of me.

He cared very deeply for people. Once I was afraid because I had found some lumps on my neck and I thought I might have Hodgkin's disease. I was very nervous, and the day I was going in for tests, I called Uncle Bobby and he told me he'd been up all night reading about Hodgkin's. He was that kind of friend. He was worried about me and so he wanted to read up on what it might be. It turned out to be benign.

I learned to fly in 1988, but I quit after my dad got into an accident and after a couple of my friends were killed in a crash. I just couldn't do it any longer.

I once asked Uncle Bobby how he could keep flying, and he said he flew because he loved it so much. He could fly every day.

In August of 1999 I decided to go back to flying. I didn't want my dad to know because I didn't want him to get excited in case I didn't stick with it. Well, Uncle Bobby almost let the secret out. After I soloed in November, I told my dad.

Uncle Bob was probably one of the most cautious pilots I know. If it was too windy, he'd head back. This one day in December, it was too hazy, but he and I took off. Once we were in the air, we turned around. "Why bother?" he would say. "You can go up on a better day."

On January 16, not long before Uncle Bobby's accident, I wanted to go up. Uncle Bobby said we'd fly out of Waukegan. He'd do one leg and I'd do the one back. So I asked my dad if he wanted to come with, but he said no. I really wanted him to come along, so we got him to do it. I'm so happy we did because it's the last time we were all together.

Something happened on that flight that was interesting. I was flying back when this plane started goofing around with us. This guy got really close to our plane, flew in front of us. He was making me really nervous. I reached back and took Uncle Bob's hand. It's what I needed at that moment.

I was feeling really bad and I made a bad landing, but when we got out, Uncle Bobby said everything was really good. He was like that. He made you feel good about whatever you did, even if you knew it wasn't your best.

After the memorial service, Chris' sister told me that I need to think I have an angel watching out for me. And I do. Uncle Bob is now my angel.

Bob and the B-17: A Respect for History

Tom Poberezny

Tom Poberezny is president of the Experimental Aircraft Association in Oshkosh, Wisconsin.

Bob served on our board of directors for about 10 years.

He came up every summer during our convention, too. The convention lasts about seven days and draws three-quarters of a million people, and 12,000 airplanes. It's a massive event. Every evening we have a program we call theater in the woods. The idea stems from World War II, when they would have these outdoor theater events to entertain the troops.

We have this big wooded area. We built a stage and have lights. We can accommodate 6,000 or 7,000 people. People bring blankets and lawn chairs. We've had Paul Harvey, Neil Armstrong, entertainers. It's the end of the day wrap-up.

Bob would come up on the weekend. He was the host and emcee. With Bob, what you see is what you get. The crowd and he interact, as opposed to just having someone up there talking to the crowd. He's with people he enjoyed. You know, aviation and motorcycling were his true loves, alongside broadcasting.

A lot of people knew him because he touched people all over the country through the reach of WGN.

So, he was an active participant as a member of our association, and as a pilot, and as a personality. He was involved, not just coming to the convention, but involved on a year-round basis in our programs.

I learned something very important about Bob after he died. I heard so many stories of how he touched people. I remember the story about the young mother whose daughter was saved because she had heard about the Heimlich maneuver on Bob show. It's amazing the impact he had.

When Bob retired from the board two years ago, he was eligible for a very special award we give out to anyone who has served at least 10 years. We have a ceremony and Bob was to have become a director emeritus. That was to be done at our spring meeting in 1999. Two days before the meeting, Scott Anderson, a close friend of Bob's, was killed in an airplane in Duluth, Minnesota. He went to the funeral, so he missed his induction as a director emeritus.

We were going to do the ceremony a year later, but, of course, he was killed before we could do it. We had just corresponded with him to confirm the details.

Another thing about Bob—he was so willing to come up here and put a face to the name. You always wonder what a voice looked like. People were so enamored of him because he was so regular.

Bob would come out there with his beard and a hat on. He'd be wearing a pair of shorts with a big jungle pocket on the side. There was no pretension. People felt better about Bob after they saw him because they realized he was just like them. Even though you might hear that on the radio, you still put him on a pedestal. Until you meet him, then he's so regular. That laugh of his started from his belly and worked its way up.

Bob loved to fly, especially in the past few years. He bought a number of airplanes. He was so excited when he came here and got a chance to fly a B-17. Now, a B-17 is a four-engine bomber from World War II. What touched Bob about this is that they're very rare, maybe only 10 or 12 of them in the world, even though there were thousands built.

Roy Stanek

They also tell a story, not just about the airplane, but the men and women who flew them. Bob was a real emotional person, a people person. That experience flying the airplane was amazing to me because he wasn't just excited about flying this old airplane, he was excited to understand that this is what it was like 50 years ago to be flying in World War II. He could understand these men. They were young men, 19, 20, 21 years old. It allowed him to put himself into a place of history that he revered and respected, not because of the tragedy of war, but because of what those people did.

That experience flying the B-17 pulled together three parts of Bob Collins—his love of flying, the excitement of flying something rare and unique, and the emotional side of what that airplane represented.

It was interesting to watch it unveil. He was like a little kid. He was excited, but he spent the time to think what it really meant.

We have a lot of veterans who get into the B-17, and it takes them back to their younger days. Bob didn't connect that way. He connected in realizing what these people did for us. It gave him a perspective of what it was like to be there.

The talent he had was the ability to get something into perspective and then sharing that with his audience.

Bob met Christine in Oshkosh. Christine's maiden name is Barton. Her dad, Jim Barton, was an American Airlines pilot and a longtime aviator in Illinois. Jim was on our board and an active member for years, until he died. It was through EAA that Bob and Christine met. She was with the airline industry, too. She was a flight attendant with TWA.

Chris grew up in an aviation family. Bob loved to fly. It all came together.

One last thought: I knew Bob through our aviation relationship. I wasn't a part of his local sphere. When I went to his funeral, I was sitting in the church. Many people spoke. I knew some of their names, others I didn't know, but I could relate to their stories.

The thing I came away with is that Bob truly was Chicago. He's the guy you woke up with in the morning, drank your coffee with, drove to work with. I listened to Bob up here in Oshkosh.

As much as I thought I knew how much he loved Chicago, I didn't realize it until then. Much more than Mike Ditka or anybody else, Bob was Chicago. His style was very Chicago. I know he was worried when he had to replace Wally Phillips 'cause Wally had a totally different style. Wally was loved by Chicago, too. But people loved Bob because of his demeanor and style, because he was just like them.

A Passion for Freedom and the Outdoors

Paul Poberezny

Paul Poberezny is chairman of the board of the Experimental Aircraft Association, in Oshkosh, Wisconsin.

Around 1976, we were building a full-sized replica of the Spirit of St. Louis. Vern Jobst was a friend of Bob, and Vern was working with me on this replica. As a result, I got to know Bob.

He'd come up and watch us building the airplane. We were going to 29 states with it, the same route as Lindbergh did in 1928, to promote aviation. Through that, we got better acquainted, and Bob got interested in aviation. He'd talk about it on the show, and Vern and I were on his program a number of times. When we actually did the flight, Bob joined us on a number of the legs, as a passenger. Mostly Vern flew, but sometimes I did. We had a lot of fun, good fellowship. Bob was always outgoing. I'm kind of the same way, so we struck up a good friendship.

He was interested in Harleys, and I am, too. We decided to take a trip out West. This was around 1982 or 1983. We went to South Dakota, up to Rapid City, into the mountains, Yellowstone, all through there.

We really enjoyed each other's company. One time I had problem with my motorcycle. We rode it to a small town to get it fixed. I think it was Sioux Falls. The mechanic didn't tighten up one of the nuts on the axle, and when I started back on it, the axle twisted. We couldn't get it undone. We were mad, but it gave us a lot of laughs, too.

We stayed close friends, went out to dinner. Through our friendship, Bob go to know Jim Barton, who is Christine's dad. That's how he met and got to know Christine.

Bob had an infectious laugh. He was a free spirit who knew how to talk with people. Sometimes he'd be a little gruff, which we all do, but he treated people with wisdom and respect.

I never heard him use foul language. He never made people feel humble.

What we shared was a love of motorcycles and airplanes. I have seven airplanes, and I like my motorcycle equally. With the motorcycle, we talked about the freedom that we had. It's like people who ride horses; you're comfortable on the road.

His love was motorcycles until he got into aviation. Motorcycling and flying are pretty similar. Both involve a love of the outdoors and freedom. You can look over the nose of an airplane and see the beauty of the earth. Same with a motorcycle; you can look through your windshield and see the beauty all around you.

When you're in an airplane, you don't feel alone; you feel privileged to enjoy this vast museum under you—the world. I had a home in Steamboat, Colorado, and one day my wife and I were flying. We were near Ogalala, Nebraska. I told her, "Hon, I've been flying more than 50 years, and I've really been flying over a museum."

I started getting books on Western history, took my motorcycle and visited these communities I never knew existed. With imagination, you can see 100 years back. Bob had that same feeling. We talked about that.

Motorcycles and Omelets

John Filopous

John Filopous is an owner of Highland House, a meeting place for motorcycle fanatics, including Bob Collins.

I liked Bob Collins. He was a nice guy, a gentleman. He would stop here on Sundays with his wife, Chris. They would ride motorcycles here. He'd order eggs, the usual stuff.

There would be 300 to 700 people here, at least, especially on a nice day.

Bob always liked sports. We have a lot of people from Chicago who ride their motorcycles here. That started about 40 years ago. Motorcycles come here all the time. It's easy for people to get here. They're not wild. People are very nice.

Bob was not the leader; he was just one of the guys. He'd spend a lot of time outside talking to people. It was fun for him. Like a sport, like anything else. Anything you do, you enjoy.

Bob Collins (far left) and his biker friends

Flying as the Great Leveler

Clark Weber

Clark Weber is president of Clark Weber Associates, a radio and television advertising agency in Chicago. He does a morning show at WAIT-AM in Chicago.

Our paths crossed professionally at various functions. My wife, Joan, and Christine got to know know each other, but I really knew Bob because we had flying as a mutual hobby.

We talked about flying whenever we got together. We both flew out of Palwaukee Airport. I used to own several planes, but sold them six or seven years ago. I've just been renting since then.

We would run into each other at Palwaukee and say we had to go flying together some day, but we never had a chance.

There's a great relationship between an individual and an airplane. An airplane doesn't respect who you are, how much you make; there's no adoration there. It is simply you and the machine. The machine demands that it be flown in a certain way; otherwise it will bite you.

Bob and I both found that flying was a great leveler of our perspectives. In this business, sometimes public adoration can swell your head. Flying makes you realize just how insignificant you really are.

I gave a talk not long ago at the Museum of Broadcasting in Chicago, on my changing from becoming an air personality to starting my own advertising agency. I looked out into the audience and

Clark Weber

there was Bob. He was quite taken by what I did and told me that was something he thought was quite special.

I think he would have moved into that direction. Like a lot of other people on the air, you realize you're tied to that umbilical cord so tightly. There's always that fear of, "Well, when the contract is over, they might not renew it."

He saw what I was doing as a way of breaking away from that radio-station dependency. He expressed admiration for it.

Chapter 8

Impact

Bob Collins: A Vanishing Breed

John Landecker

John Records Landecker is the morning host on WJMK, 104.3 FM in Chicago.

The first time I ever met Bob Collins, he was working afternoons at WGN. I was working afternoons at WLUP, the Loop.

Both of us were doing our shows at Chicagofest near the bandshell. I was walking up and down the promenade and we met, had a nice chat.

I don't remember him being inappropriately dressed. I worked with Larry Lujack, who is the original bad dresser. Anything compared to Uncle Lar is a step up. My experience with radio people is that they universally have no regard for their clothing. Seeing someone on the

John Records Landecker
Oldies 104·3 WJMK

radio dressed very casually is something I wouldn't notice.

He did have a beard, I know that, and was very friendly.

I think Bob Collins is important to radio, honestly, because of the type of radio practiced by WGN. That type of radio is important regardless of who's doing it. It's a community-oriented, friendly, nonconfrontational, informative, entertainment format, which is very successful. Those types of radio programs across the country are few and far between.

It's my opinion that radio in this country was intended to be like that, the kind of radio the FCC meant for America to be listening to: radio stations that are involved in their communities, inform them, and entertain them. That's the kind of radio I grew up on. That's the kind of radio station, on a small level, that I went to work for when I was in high school.

My first job was as a janitor at a station outside of Ann Arbor, Michigan; that was one of these full-service radio stations—talk shows, newscasts, business reports, and that type of thing. That, plus rock 'n' roll music, drew me to radio.

The first radio stations, even rock 'n' roll stations, had a great degree of community involvement and news, which they don't anymore.

The landscape has changed completely, making the type of radio that Bob Collins and WGN do more important to me. While they are a zillion, million, rock stations with less talk and more music, and shock radio is everywhere, there simply aren't that many stations doing the WGN style of radio. That's sort of sad.

I think the laws that were passed that allow one corporation to own as many stations as they want in this country is a detriment to the quality of radio the public is getting. The people who run radio stations are on the air to benefit the stockbrokers who have stock I that company, not the listeners.

Bob Collins was on the radio to benefit the listener, to address the needs of the people in this community.

The attraction of Bob as an individual was that he was the same person on the air as he was when he started. He maintained his small-town innocence to the very end, and it wasn't phony. Chicago has seen many people come to town, become successful and think they're the center of the universe.

Bob was not one of those. Bob was a vanishing breed. I'm afraid we won't see too many more like him because the corporate structure today doesn't promote that type of radio. It's expensive to do. It requires money to staff a show with traffic, weather, helicopters, engineers. Quite few people work on that show. Anything that costs money today is something radio owners don't want to do.

Willing to Support a Stranger

Garry Meier

Garry Meier has been a radio personality in Chicago since 1973. A native of Chicago, he is now afternoon talk show host on WLS AM.

In the fall of 1993, I had just gone through this acrimonious break-up with my former partner. I had just started doing my own show on WLUP. A couple of months into my show, I got a call. My producer said it was Bob Collins.

I'd never met him, and I didn't know what he thought of my other show.

I remember he said, "Hey, this is Bob Collins. I've been listening to your new show. I like it. I know it's been a tough time for you, but keep going."

I didn't know the guy, and I thought that was a nice gesture.

It was out of nowhere. I heard after he died that he liked doing that. He was very supportive of people, even people he didn't know.

There's a lot of venom in this business, and I thought it was interesting that Bob Collins didn't have that venom. This business is so competitive and weird, but this guy wasn't.

I always appreciated that phone call.

I got a call from one of his co-workers a couple of days after he died. This co-worker said the last conversation he had with Bob was the morning of his death. This guy asked Bob, "Have you ever listened to Roe and Garry on WLS?"

And Bob said, "Those guys have really come a long way. It sounds really good."

He didn't care that it was the competition. If he liked you, he told you. He seemed to be very honest in his feelings about people.

The style of radio he was doing is not the style that other people do in this market. He wasn't acerbic; he had a different agenda. And he did it very well.

He Could Make Anything Interesting

Gus Azinger

Gus Azinger lives in Wautoma, Wisconsin, and produces marketing videos.

I used to write commercials. One of my commercials was a series of 10-second spots for the Seven Mile Fair. We placed them on WGN on a random schedule, cheaper that way. The only way you knew they were running was to listen.

This one morning, Bob had Burt Reynolds on as a guest. They were chatting live on the air. Collins said to Burt: "Weren't you in radio before you went into movies?" Reynolds says, "I was a jock down in Texas. I haven't been behind a mic in many years."

So Collins says, "When's the last time you did a commercial?" Reynolds says, "I can't even remember." Collins shuffles some paper, and you hear him say, "Try this one, it's a short one."

So Reynolds reads the commercial for Seven Mile Fair, which was something like, "Where can you find a dozen eggs or a darning egg? Seven Mile Fair. Just south of Milwaukee, on I-94. Open 12 hours a day, Saturday and Sunday."

Reynolds finishes and says, "What the hell is a darning egg?"

Well, you can imagine Collins is thinking about that one. "I think it has something to do with sewing up holes in socks," he says. "We'll go to the listeners. Anybody want to call in?"

While they're waiting for the first call, Reynolds says, "What is this place, Seven Mile Fair?"

Collins says, "It's one of the biggest flea markets I've ever seen. It's phenomenal."

I was in my car, and I almost drove off the road.

They talked with listeners about that darning egg and that Seven Mile Fair for 20 minutes, and I was a hero to my clients. It was kind of neat that Bob did that. He could talk about anything and make it interesting.

A King among Kings

Eric Zorn

Eric Zorn is a metro news columnist for the Chicago Tribune, *and appeared regularly as a guest on Bob Collins' program. He wrote a column about the radio industry for the* Tribune *from 1982 to 1985.*

I disagreed with those who hailed Bob after his death as a ground-breaking figure or the last of certain breed. And I mean no disrespect by that assessment, with which I suspect he would agree.

Bob was, instead, the deserving head that wore the crown and ruled (all too briefly) over the important kingdom that is Chicago radio. This town has a great tradition of radio monarchs—hosts who really mattered to the civic life here—and it's almost impossible to rank them against one another. They have been, traditionally, unique—not pale imitations of their predecessors—and Bob was no exception.

Was he better for his time and for his audience than Wally Phillips, Howard Miller, or the others? More important than Steve Dahl, Clark Weber or Larry Lujack? Not even ratings books can begin to answer that question.

What one can say for sure is that Bob was a very worthy heir to Wally Phillips and that if the form holds, his successors will prove worthy heirs to him.

Culture Shock for WGN and Its Listeners

Bruce DuMont

Bruce DuMont is president of the Museum of Broadcast Communications in Chicago. He was the original producer of Extension 720 and also produced the Marty McNeeley Saturday Night Special, WGN Sports Central, and the Howard Miller show, all for WGN.

To me, Bob is important because he represents a transitional figure in the history of WGN radio, which is probably the most

Bruce DuMont

important radio station in the history of Chicago because of its reach and its success.

It certainly over the years has vied with WLS and WBBM for the type of dominance a station with 50,000-watt power probably has. Because you're on WGN, you're instantly important, but it doesn't instantly make you a success.

Bob Collins is an important transitional figure because he helped change the sound of the radio station. When he got there, it was almost exclusively a bastion for deep-throated baritone announcers whose careers began in the '30s and '40s and who had a certain sound about them: Franklyn MacCormack, John Mallow, Carl Greyson.

There certainly was nobody on the station who sounded like Bob Collins when he got there. He had a Southern twang, a crackle in his voice, down-home on a station that was decidedly not down-home.

The fact that Bob Henley hired him was itself something of a revolutionary decision by the station. Bob Henley came from rural roots and so perhaps the sound of Bob Collins' voice and his demeanor was not as off-putting as it was to some people at Tribune Tower initially. He didn't even sound like a radio announcer.

I was working at WGN at the time, and there were a lot of people who didn't think Collins was going to make it because it was too much of a culture shock, not only for the people at the radio, but for the people of Chicago, too.

The show Bob replaced was called Music Unlimited, which was hosted by John Mallow. It was a scripted one-hour music show that I produced and also wrote. That's what you have to understand when you realize what Bob was taking over. It would be like Willie Nelson or Charlie Daniels going to perform before the Chicago Symphony Orchestra. That would be the culture shock he represented.

Bob started in the 7 p.m. shift, which is where I would run into him from time to time. He was different on the air, off the air. Most of the announcers would have shirts and ties and finely creased pants. Bob would show up with Levis and cowboy boots and checkered shirts, his crackling voice, scratching himself. It was just culture shock.

Wally Phillips was dominant in the morning, and when he decided to step aside, it was logical for the station to try Bob Collins. In radio, morning drive time is the number-one slot to be in, followed by evening drive time. Everybody held their breath about whether Bob would be acceptable to Wally's audience, which was a little bit older, staid, and WGN traditional.

It proved out to be a brilliant move because he inherited Wally's phenomenal audience and expanded it. He continued to be tops in the ratings until the day he died.

The sad thing is he didn't match Wally in overall ratings as far as longevity only because of the tragedy of his death. Wally was number one for 15 to 20 years. Bob was number one for a shorter period of time.

Shaking Hands with a Legend

Art Hellyer

Art Hellyer lives in Naperville, Illinois, and is a legend in radio. He worked for WIND, WMAQ, WGN, WBBM, WLS, WLS-FM, WJJD, and channels 2, 5, 7, and 9. He was the ABC television network announcer for 30 years.

I did thousands of commercials over the years for Ford Motor Company, Standard Oil, AT&T.

We would record those at WGN-TV. I shared Ray Raynard's dressing room. I didn't have one because I was a freelancer. Ray came up to me one day and said, "Art, you're here so much, share my dressing room with me. We've been friends for years."

I would see Bob Collins in the building because this was when the radio and television were in the same building. Well, one day Bob stopped me in the hall.

He came up to me and introduced himself, shook my hand, and said something about wanting to meet me because I was a legend and I'd done so much. He said, "You and Arthur Godfrey did so much to open radio for the rest of us. I wanted to thank you."

I was pleased and surprised. If you ever watched *Maverick, My Three Sons, Wide World of Sports, Monday Night Football,* or so many other programs, I was the announcer. I did the opens and closes, commercials, bumpers, everything.

I listened to Bob over the years and I found him, well, for one thing he was clean. That's very important to me. I've been in radio for 53 years. I've never said "hell" or "damn" on the air. I don't believe in that sort of thing. You didn't have to worry about the kids listening to you.

He had a wonderful sense of humor, but he could be cutting, too. People enjoyed him tremendously.

He came across in everybody's home as what he was, just a good guy.

You know that old song, "What It Was Was Football," was a favorite of Bob.

I have a photo of myself with Andy Griffith when he was going around with that record. Andy Griffith was a great stand-up comedian, and that song was really popular, around 1953.

Well, Bob would talk about his "big orange," and that came right out of that record.

Chapter 9

•••••••

Fans and Listeners

Roy Stanek

Bob Collins enjoyed meeting his fans.

He Took Away the Loneliness

Judith E. A. Perkinson

Judith E. A. Perkinson is the president of The Calumet Group, Inc., a business training firm in Hammond, Indiana.

What is the measure of a man? Our society places value on any number of factors. How rich he is, how smart he is, how handsome he is, how famous he is, or how powerful he is. But those factors tend to be important when he is living. Many of these factors are predicated on that person's potential value to you as an individual. What he can do for you, and what you can get from him.

What about when he is dead? Then what is the measure of a man? When he is dead the measure of a man is how he touched this world, what he did with his talent, his intelligence, and his money, and how what he did touched the world around him. All that remain are our memories. Now, the memories give us insight into the real mark he made on the world.

This is the story of how Bob Collins touched the life of one man. Bill Myres was 82 years old when Bob Collins died. He is blind and lives alone. He is my father. My dad is fiercely independent, and when my mother died six years ago, Dad was determined he would learn to live on his own, and he did! We arranged for his meals and a cleaning lady. My husband and I always go out to eat on Friday evening with Dad. He even learned to cook. Of course, we would be there as much as we could, but even so, that left a lot of empty hours when he would be alone. We could find ways to meet his physical needs but the truth of the matter was, he was alone and our worst enemy was loneliness.

When my mom was alive, if you asked my parents what radio station they listened to, the response would be WGN. This has been true for decades. After all, WGN is the home of the Cubs, and the Cubs are an institution in our family. We could have enjoyed a World Series if they had only used my father to "manage the team."

The day would begin with the radio tuned to the morning show. At first it was Wally Phillips, and then it was Bob Collins. My mom really liked Wally Phillips; I stood in line one year to get him to sign his book so I could give her an autographed copy for Christmas.

Mom's first response to Bob Collins was not positive. He was not Wally Phillips. My dad did not share that opinion. For him "Uncle Bobby" was a breath of fresh air. In those days Wally and Bob were little more than radio personalities to my folks. If either of them had suddenly died, it would have been sad, but it would not have been experienced as a personal loss.

How time can change things. When we heard the news about the plane crash, our first thoughts were for my father. Two different friends called to ask me if I had heard the news about Bob Collins and how my dad was. How could a radio personality have such an impact on a person's life? I guess you would have to understand the relationship Dad had with Bob Collins.

To begin with, my father never called into the show; he never spoke with Bob Collins, and he never met him in person. And yet Bob Collins was my dad's very personal friend. I worry a great deal about my father, but I never worried about him in the morning. In the morning he was never alone; he was with Bob Collins.

After my mother died, Dad had to find his own routine. For a while it was hard. He seemed to sleep too much and had his days and nights mixed up. Being blind, there was little to distinguish day from night. Then he got into the habit of listening to Bob Collins in the morning. I don't want to sound melodramatic, but it gave him something to get up for in the morning.

Bob Collins helped my Dad stabilize a routine. Mornings were spent with Uncle Bobby. The radio went on as soon as he was up and the dialogue began. Oh, Bob Collins didn't have the benefit of both sides of the conversation, but believe me the conversation was two-sided. The cleaning lady would hear him talking away in the kitchen and think someone had come into the house, only to find him talking to the radio.

Dad's relationship with Bob Collins was very real and very personal. Often I would get a call asking me if I had heard such and such that Bob Collins had said. I'd like a dime for every time Dad would say, "Did you hear Bob Collins this morning?" or "Bob Collins thinks…." I really didn't listen to the Collins show, but I sure got a bunch of it secondhand.

The topics discussed on the Collins show were often the source of an afternoon phone conversation between Dad and his friend Mark. Our traditional Friday-evening dinner out would almost always include something that was brought up by Uncle Bobby. He might as well have been a part of our family.

The Collins show was my dad's window to the world. It gave him something to talk about, and it brought him closer to what was going on outside his limited world. I recognized this need in my dad and thought he might really enjoy the in-depth reporting of National Public Radio. I was sure it would fill this need better than Bob Collins. I was wrong. It was not about the information; it was about how he got the information.

He could listen to news all day if he wanted to, but it would not have filled the need he had for companionship. Bob Collins filled that need in the morning. Every morning. Dad once said, "He is my friend. But, think about it, how many friends do you get to see every day? I get to see Bob Collins every day." A powerful insight from a blind man.

When Bob Collins was suddenly snatched away from this Earth we felt great sympathy for his family, but we worry about my dad. This is a serious loss for my father. It is as real as if a member of our family had died. He has not done well with the loss. There is a serious void. The sunshine in the morning is gone, and he is alone again.

As painful as the loss has been, I am eternally grateful for what Bob Collins did for my dad. He reached out over the airwaves and touched my dad's heart. He gave dad a reason to get up in the morning. He gave him a window to the world. He made Dad laugh. He made Dad cry. He took away the loneliness. Most of all he took away the loneliness.

Roy Stanek

God Bless you Bob Collins.

Waking up with Bob

Marie Hendrixon

Marie Hendrixon lives in New Era, Michigan.

Bob made me laugh and think and care. In the morning! I'm not a morning person, but when the clock radio went off, I at least wanted to listen to Bob 'til I could actually wake up.

The best was when the radio turned on during one of his so recognizable laughs. Lord, I miss that laugh. Or his "blaming" Lyle or Tom for the traffic being late because of their newscast running too long. Of course it was never Bob's fault!

You couldn't help but smile even if not fully awake. I'd drag myself to the kitchen and turn on that radio on my way to wake a kid, then the bathroom radio would go on as I brushed my teeth and got ready for the day.

Despite being at the top for so long and no doubt having oodles of money, Bob seemed like someone you could have lunch with and talk to as a regular person. That came through the radio; it was like he was speaking right to you. It didn't matter if he was talking to some bigwig or a person who had lost a dog or had a family member that had wandered off; you wanted to listen because he was really interested in the person. Even if someone was really ticking him off, he was always under control while letting his views be known.

The news of his death was unbelievable. I kept hoping he would call and say, "Hey, guys! Are you kidding? I'm fine." But precisely because neither he nor Christine called in, I knew it was true. I cried many times that first hard week with the WGN family.

I'm not positive just when I started listening to Bob. I moved out-of-state in 1979 and started listening to WGN a few years later when WLS and WCFL changed formats. I had listened to my Cubs and just started leaving it on more and more. I've been divorced for a while now, so I was waking up with Bob longer than I did with a husband.

I still miss hearing him.

As Comfortable as an Old Shoe

Jeneane Webster

Jeneane Webster lives in Michigan City, Indiana, with her three teens.

Bob Collins' laughter made me happy. Sometimes his laughter made me cry. It made me cry because he made me happy. Go figure. I cry at Charmin commercials…I think this falls under the "hurts so good" category.

I have always wondered how I could feel so close to someone I never really knew. How could I feel so befriended by someone who spoke to me through a box nearly every day for 25 years? Somehow this man was an integral part of my real life. I have no idea how many times I quoted him to my friends, family, and co-workers. I should have been on commission for WGN for all the free publicity I gave that station. I actually got listeners for them because of my love for Bob Collins. These weren't one-time listeners. They listen to the station to this day.

I used to speak to my grandmother daily, and we always shared Bob Collins stories. She would fill me in on what happened after I had gone in to work. After she died, I found myself thinking, I should call her and tell her something humorous Bob had said or done. Now I have two tremendous voids in my life.

Remember how Bob always hated himself on "the T and V"? I remember seeing him during an auto show broadcast prior to his marriage to Christine, "his bride." He moved Chris to the front of the camera and introduced her. It was such a kind and gentle gesture. I'll never forget it. I knew I liked her because of her "non-stardom-seeking" demeanor. It was obvious to a viewer how much they cared about one another. And how they complemented each other. He was the original "non-stardom-seeker."

I met Bob once. It was probably in 1983 or '84 at Chicago Fest. My daughter was a toddler, and I asked him if she could have a "Big Orange Cap." He said he couldn't give her one. I thanked him and walked away. As I was leaving the area, I realized I had not even bothered to tell him how very much I enjoyed him and his show. I was so embarrassed at my behavior. I remember trying to explain this to my husband and suggesting we go back so I could correct the blunder. He felt I was being foolish, so I let it go. Sure wish I had followed my own instinct. Shoulda, woulda, coulda.

Every June 3rd, I think of Billy Jo McAllister jumping off the Tallahassee Bridge. I remember "Papa Was a Rolling Stone." Bobby Goldsboro's "Summer the First Time." My ex-husband is ten years my junior, so that song has a very special meaning.

Bob Collins made me cry every year on Martin Luther King's birthday, Robert Kennedy's birthday, John Kennedy's birthday, when he played "Abraham, Martin, and John," Or when he played "What the World Needs Now," the version with the interviews by the children. Or Elvis' rendition of "The Battle Hymn of the Republic." He made me cry by sharing his raw emotions. His feelings were so close to the surface I believe you could have reached out and touched them.

I'm an animal lover. So was he. I very vividly recall the day he had to have one of his dogs put down. He was so shaken that he could not do his show. He left midair and let Chuck Swirski finish the show. Collins never worried about the "manly" thing to do. He did what he felt. That was what set him apart from others. He was so natural, so true, and so tender. Emotions worked for him. He didn't have to work at emotions.

Who hasn't thought about his telling his dad he loved him? Those four words, "I love you, Daddy" have probably reached out and touched more people than any phone commercial ever could have accomplished. I practiced that long enough with my own father that finally, after years of having to ask my father if he loved me, he now voluntarily ends every phone call and/or visit with "I love you." My father is 76 and I am 54. So many wasted years.

I loved his repetitive lines. Laughin' and scratchin'. I use it daily. My favorite line was, "A horse walks into a bar, and the bartender says, why the long face?" It cracks me up every time I hear

Roy Stanek

Bob always attracted a crowd of admirers.

or use it. What really cracks me up is the look on one of my victims' faces when I say it. Most have *no* clue what I'm talking about. That is what is so great. You always had to pay attention to Bob to understand what he was talking about, and I am the same way. If you snooze, you lose.

He never failed to make me laugh when referring to the Memo Fairy. After hearing that reference, I quickly incorporated it into my work dialogue. I use it to this day. His irreverent attitude toward the upper echelon was just another trait that showed his genuine soul. He was normal. He was you, he was me. Yet he was so very proud to be a part of the WGN family. How many times did he say he loved his work and he got paid for doing something he loved so much?

Bob Collins was a one-of-a-kind guy. He will never be replaced. He was as spontaneous as his laughter. He was as Irish as Paddy's behind. He was as comfortable as an old shoe. I loved him as though I knew him intimately all my life. We had history: 25 years of it.

He Made it Okay to Laugh Again

Judi Jelinek

Judi Jelinek worked for West Group, a law-book publisher, for 30 years. She divides her time between homes in Wisconsin and Lake Villa, Illinois.

A couple of years ago, my daughter suddenly died. My world was forever changed, and I felt that I would never be happy again. A few hazy days later, I happened to actually be hearing the radio that was always on in the morning. Bob was on the air. And he made me laugh. I knew then that although my life was forever changed, I could go on, and I could laugh and enjoy life again.

When Bob left us, I felt that once again my world as I knew it was askew. I knew that there were many people devastated by his loss and countless others saddened to know we would never wake up to "Uncle Bobby" again.

Recently I was talking with a friend. We were discussing our lives and what twists and turns they had taken from our childhood dreams. I came away feeling that although I am content with whom and where I am today, I really haven't made a difference in this world. I mentioned this to my children, who informed me that I had made a difference in their lives and their worlds.

We had this discussion the day after Bob Collins died, and it set me to thinking about the difference he made in so many lives, including my own.

Bob was always there for me in the morning while I got ready for and traveled to work. His voice was as comforting as my favorite coffee mug and my old squishy slippers. Sometimes he made me angry, often he made me think, and mostly he made me laugh.

To those of you who are Bob's family and friends, know how much he was loved. Know how much he made a difference in so many of our lives. Know that you will laugh and live again, as he showed me after such a loss. He made a difference, and that is a wonderful legacy we can embrace. He made a difference. Thank you, Bob.

Listening on the Internet

Frank L. Van De Vanter

Frank L. Van De Vanter lives in Berwyn, a Chicago suburb. He is a computer-support professional.

I grew up listening to WGN, living in the western suburbs of Chicago. I remember listening to Bob in the afternoon, after grade school and all through my high-school years.

Today, as I listen to Spike O'Dell in the morning, I remember why, after growing up listening to Wally Phillips, I continued to listen to WGN when Bob took the morning reins. He never failed to make me laugh on a daily basis, and his friendly pokes at his staff and friends will never be forgotten.

After Bob took over the morning drive time, I struggled getting him on the radio. I was working in downtown Chicago, where signal problems are well-known.

The commercialization of the Internet in the '90s allowed me to listen to Bob anywhere I was traveling. If not for Uncle Bob, I would have given up on AM radio.

I don't think he realized the listener strength that he had through the Internet nationally and internationally.

I was on his Pop Quiz

Bette Gutantes

Bette Gutantes is a listener from Gurnee, Illinois.

I was unprepared for my reaction to the loss of Bob Collins. It really hit me so hard. Sadness filled me. I hadn't realized what a part of my morning Bob and WGN had become. What was it that touched me so much?

He was, after all, just a "radio guy." As I thought about it, I realized he was "my radio guy." I felt some ownership in him and his show. As my radio alarm would go off, his was the first voice I would hear each morning. My awareness of myself, as I awoke each day, was mixed with him. Senses are powerful. They linked me to him in an almost unconscious way. When the sound, the laugh, the cadence and rhythm of his voice were gone, I felt a loss, and still do. His voice became a feeling of attachment to the morning, a comfort, a habit, just as the aroma and flavor of that first cup of coffee. Things just don't feel quite right in the morning anymore.

I listened for more conscious reasons, too. I just plain liked him. He was an Irish Catholic, as am I, and seemed like family. He made you feel like you knew him. He made you think, feel, wonder, question, and, of course, laugh.

I was fortunate to have met Bob once in 1997 when I was a teacher on his Pop Quiz. When I knew our school was picked to be on, I really wanted to be one of the teachers selected, and made that known to all at school that day. Another teacher, also a "Bob fan," and I were chosen to represent our school, and we couldn't have been more excited. Meeting Bob and being on his show was such a great time. He was so genuine and endearing. He put us all at ease right away. I remember him saying that in no way would he embarrass us, and we should just relax. He, of course, made us laugh, with his quick wit and gentle teasing. He truly wanted us to do well and was rooting for us on every question. When we'd answer right, he'd shout, "Yessss!" I will always remember the experiences of that day and treasure my "I survived the dreaded Milt question" T-shirt, which, by the way, we got wrong. He impressed me that day as such a professional, yet he was a regular guy. I admired that combination.

Yes, he was "my radio guy." Every morning, when a vague feeling of loss wafts through my sleepy mind, I do remember, and miss him.

An Intimate Member of the Family

Bob Fiorita

Bob Fiorita is a native Chicagoan (West Side), and a die-hard Cubs, Bears, Bulls, Blackhawks, and DePaul fan. His wife, Julie, is a native of Milwaukee. They now live and work in Northern California.

Like many Chicagoans, I grew up listening to WGN radio. My earliest recollections, however, don't relate to Cubs baseball or Bears football broadcasts but to the hypnotic voice of Franklyn MacCormack on late-night radio reciting poetry or some lyric from a romantic piece of 1940s music. My mother listened to Franklyn MacCormack late at night in 1946 to soothe the pain of her loneliness.

As a child and even as a teenager in the 1950s, television was not a prominent part of life as it is today. WGN radio was one of the places I visited with my imagination. In those days, I came home from school in the afternoon to catch the latest episode of *The Lone Ranger, Superman* or *Jack Armstrong, the All-American Boy*. During weekday evenings, I did my homework while my mother ironed clothes, as we listened to the *Lux Theater* or *Fibber Magee and Molly* or *The Shadow*.

In 1964, because of my job, I spent a lot of time in my car, travelling the Chicago metropolitan area. WGN kept me company throughout the day. Wally Phillips started the day and, after coming to Chicago from Boston, Roy Leonard took care of the rest of the morning. From March through October, baseball took up most afternoons. When the Cubs weren't playing, or during rain delays, I listened to Bill Berg in the afternoon slot. That was the place in the program schedule, when new radio personalities seemed to break into the WGN lineup. In 1975, that's where I first heard Bob Collins.

I had to adjust to Bob Collins. It wasn't that I disliked him at first. But Bob Collins was different. First of all he had this laugh. I don't know how to describe that Bob Collins laugh or even if it is

Bob Collins in 1982

capable of being described. Bob Collins' laugh is something you just have to experience. Then there's the rock-'n'-roll thing.

Wally did trivia stuff about movies and Ellery Queen mysteries. Roy did classic interviews with Jim Croce and Carly Simon and James Taylor and Harry Chapin. Bill Berg talked sports. Bob Collins was a reformed rock-'n'-roll deejay. He did trivia about rock 'n' roll. The WGN radio Barn Dance halls must have shook at the time. And Bob Collins started talking about other things like politics and flying and riding Harley Hogs. Wally never talked about his hobbies. (I saw Wally at a driving range once in Libertyville without his hair and in dark Bermuda shorts with black socks and dark shoes. I understood and respected why Wally didn't talk about his hobbies.) Bob Collins kind of grew on you.

Career decisions led to my wife and I moving first to Minneapolis in 1984 and then to Southern California in 1987. When we moved back to Chicago in 1989, we set the morning wake-up alarm to 720 on the AM radio dial. Of course, I expected to hear Wally Phillips' voice greet me that first morning in February.

Much to my surprise, Bob Collins was there instead. Again, I had to make another adjustment. Wally was king of morning radio. My father listened to Wally Phillips every morning as he traveled to his job as a CTA foreman at one of the bus garages in the city. In 1974 I called Wally at 6 a.m. to announce the birth of our son and my dad's namesake. My friends at work called Wally to arrange ways to embarrass me before millions of Chicago radio listeners. Believe me, Bob Collins as the WGN-radio morning man required some adjustment.

But Bob Collins became Uncle Bobby. And Uncle Bobby became a regular fixture in our home as my wife and I prepared for work each day. Bob Collins was a regular guy. He was sincere. He admitted that he didn't know everything about everything. He had blemishes and faults that all of us could relate to. He had struggles and disappointments, hopes and fears. When he talked to politicians, he asked the kind of questions I would like to ask. When he talked with celebrities, he wasn't star-struck. He asked the kind of questions that I would like to have answered. He disliked pretense and hypocrisy. Bob Collins was down-to-earth and practical. He hated wearing a tie, and the tuxedo was the invention of the devil. Bob genuinely liked to talk with his parents and his sister in California. He loved his wife and their pets. And he loved to ride his Harley and fly his plane.

That's what endeared Uncle Bobby to most of us. We could relate to him because he was one of us, one of the family. Yes, Wally

Phillips and Roy Leonard are part of that WGN family, too. But Uncle Bobby was different. Uncle Bobby's show was a family affair. That is his legacy. His radio family was his family: Annie and Dave; Old Blue Eyes and Jan Coleman; the Big O and Max; the guys in the sports department; the traffic-helicopter crew and so on. They seemed to be as much a part of Uncle Bobby's family as his wife, Christine. And he made the average listener like me a welcomed member of that extended family. He did that like he did everything—in an unassuming way, never attaching any significance to himself in the process.

The term "uncle" fits Bob Collins very appropriately. He was an intimate member of the family, a relative to be loved and respected. You could have fun with and laugh with Uncle Bobby. But you could also be serious and ask for his counsel because you knew that he cared deeply and genuinely. As Uncle Bobby, Bob Collins made himself available. He was approachable, not aloof and distant.

Some rare individuals achieve greatness by doing simple, everyday things exquisitely well. The measure of how well they do what they do is that it appears to be easy. Bob Collins did what he did every day extremely well. It looked easy and effortless. Bob Collins had heroes and he talked about them and he talked with them every day, Monday through Friday, 5 to 9 a.m.

They are the heroes that go unnoticed. The guy or gal who wakes up each morning and makes a conscious decision not to use alcohol or drugs. Single parents who struggle to love and discipline their children as they teach them the values of respecting the needs and rights of others. Teachers who spend hours with our children and instill in them a lifelong love for learning and personal growth. Men and women who serve us breakfast, lunch, or dinner everyday with a smile and friendly banter in our favorite neighborhood restaurant. Men and women firefighters, paramedics and law-enforcement personnel who put their lives on the line each day for the safety and protection of others. Men and women of the clergy who guide our spiritual journey with no applause. I could go on.

This is the Bob Collins family. These are the men and women who listened to Uncle Bobby and called in to talk to him each morning.

My wife and I moved to Northern California in 1998. I was driving home from the airport after a business trip that Tuesday evening on February 8th when I heard the tragic news that WGN radio personality Bob Collins and two others died as a result of a plane crash just north of Chicago. I will always remember where I was and what I was doing when I heard that Uncle Bobby died.

My wife and I will be in Chicago in May and again in July 2000. We will listen to the Spike O'Dell radio experiment and to the WGN Love Pump family, as time will permit during our visit. In the meantime, we will continue to check in on our radio family using the Internet. We know through faith that Bob Collins has gone to a better place, but we will miss Uncle Bobby. We will miss him very much.

Bob Matured as a Farm Reporter

Bobette Von Bergen

Bobette Von Bergen lives in Hebron, Illinois. A self-described workaholic, she volunteers for almost anything. She is a retired member of the local school board and works as the treasurer of the Hebron Business Association.

Time has passed since that day when two planes collided in midair, killing three. It was and still is a shock and a major loss in our lives, as well as those of the co-workers and families of the victims.

We were listeners of WGN for many years before Bob Collins arrived there. Being farmers, the farm report was a much-needed item in our lives, and that meant listening to WGN's farm report.

When Bob came to WGN, we thought, "Oh, he'll never fit in on this station," but soon he had grown on us and we listened whenever we could. In 1978, when we moved to our new home on the farm we bought the year before, we had an intercom put in. Of course, it was tuned to WGN. You could hear the station in every

Roy Stanek

Bob waits for divine inspiration.

room in the house. This wasn't what our nine-year-old wanted to hear, but he turned it off in his room and put up with our listening. He is now 29, farming with us, and an avid listener.

Mike belongs to an Antique Tractor Club, and we hosted its first annual Plow Day this past fall. Max Armstrong brought his Super M to the show and plowed. I had hoped to extend an invitation to Bob for this year's event. It wasn't meant to be.

Our daughter, Michelle, was born in 1979, and she survived the WGN radio station. She is in nurses' college and does listen occasionally when she is home. She e-mailed me when Bob was killed, because she knew I would be upset. We had met Bob at the Cubs convention one year; Michelle was an Andre Dawson Fan!

We listened and "heard" Bob grow, mature along with his audience over the years. At first he was opinionated and his way was right, but soon he was listening to both sides and, even if he didn't agree, he listened.

I remember cleaning and painting our tenant house to Jim and Bob doing the soap-opera thing. I almost fell off the ladder laughing with them. When the Pop Quiz was on, our school secretary entered us (at that time I was a PTO officer) in the contest and continued to enter us for many years to come. I stayed home and listened to the drawings of the schools every day and got caught up in the contest.

I remember sitting in the car one day at the grocery store, listening before I could go in and shop. One year I spent 45 minutes waiting to talk to him about pumpkins, but it was St. Patrick's Day and his producer kept coming on the line and saying, "I don't know what he is doing today." I never got to talk to him, but that was okay.

Bob seemed to know what we wanted to hear or what we needed more information on. He was like one of the family, a brother, a favorite uncle. One time when they were talking about where to get good sweet corn, a lady truck driver from our town called him and mentioned our vegetable market. He said he thought he had been there. We had a lot of our customers come in and tell us that they had heard our name mentioned by Bob Collins.

We sent him some sweet corn, but it turned out he had left for vacation that next day. He still sent a letter thanking us, and I know he didn't eat it, because he was gone. In the fall of that year a man and woman came to the stand and said their name was Von Bergen. They were doing the genealogy of the Von Bergen family and had heard our name on WGN. They drove out from the city looking for us. They are distant cousins of my husband. We were able to share some information they didn't have, and they were very happy to have found more of the family.

One day Bob left the program abruptly and no one said what had happened until the next day. Christine had found a lump in her breast (it turned out benign), and he felt he should share this with his listeners. She wasn't sure, but finally agreed. It gave me courage to call the doctor when I found a lump not too many months after that. (Mine was also benign.)

His love of his stepfather and stepmother and sister was so evident over the years, the phone calls ending with, "I love you, Daddy," and his frantic call to his sister during the earthquake or mudslides, I'm not sure which. He was ready to leave immediately to go to help her and tried to convince her to move. This was all shared with us and made us a part of his life.

This morning as we awoke to Spike and Max and the gang, Spike told a joke about robins eating their fill of worms and basking in the sun afterward. A cat came sneaking up and had Baskin' Robins. It was funny for 5 a.m., but something was missing: Bob's laugh!

Yes he was a brother, an uncle…a friend.

My Driving Companion

Anita Fishman

Anita Fishman lives in South Bend, Indiana. She is a mother, "grammy," college graduate, self-employed person, and volunteer who loves to play golf, garden, cook, read, and travel.

Time has passed, so the shock and some of the pain of the tragedy has subsided. I'm talking about the air crash and death of Bob Collins. I still miss him. The radios in the cars are still set on 720, WGN Chicago, and we live in South Bend, Indiana.

I was driving from Michigan City, Indiana, where my mom lives, that afternoon; of course, I was listening to 720 when I heard the initial report. That report was done with great dignity, sensitivity, and reserved emotion. When all was confirmed, sadness and a great feeling of loss overcame me.

My relationship with Bob Collins was only in our cars. His voice; inflection; laugh; sense of humor; choice of songs; love of children and their well-being; relationship with the people of Chicago and, obviously, other places; and his partnership with his fellow professionals at the station were some of the attributes that made me feel close to him.

He entertained and educated me while I was driving or riding in the car. Of course, I have to say that I like listening to WGN; it is on automatic, like cruise control.

But I still miss Bob.

Going to the Web Site Just to See His Face

Stu Fishman

Stu Fishman lives in South Bend, Indiana, and is vice president of sales and marketing for an English public company.

It is hard to drive to work in the morning even only for 10 minutes or so and not hear the laughter and joy of Bob Collins. He truly seemed to love everyone who called him, even if he disagreed and sometimes got very upset with callers. I admired his knowl-

Bob works the room.

Roy Stanek

edge of so many facets of life, including biking, politics, sports, family, and, of course, flying. I never met him or talked to him on the radio, although I tried a few times when the subject was familiar to me. Often, someone else called him to explain something he didn't understand before I had a chance.

I did reach his producer, who offered me the opportunity to be put on hold, but I often couldn't wait. The most recent call was to inform him of a terrible fire at the new Salvation Army store here in South Bend. The Salvation Army was Bob's favorite charity. We joined many donors in the area by giving as much as we could to replenish the store. I don't know if Bob got my message, but I felt better letting him know.

He was the most genuine person I have ever heard on news or talk radio. I frequently went to the WGN Web site just to see his face, his bearded sweet face! It must have been very amusing to see him riding his beloved bike dressed in black leather! I truly miss him.

Three Generations of Fans Laugh and Cry

David M. Hahn

David M. Hahn is division manager for Butternut Bread in Clinton, Wisconsin. He has been married to his own "old Agnes" (real name, Donna) for 23 years. They have three kids.

My parents were traveling throughout the South from about January 1 until returning home on March 5 (to rest up for further travels).

One of the first things they asked me was what happened to Uncle Bobby.

I explained what had transpired that day, and we sat and talked for a little while, reminiscing about the laughter that Bob brought to our home.

We remembered the "damn cat—why name it, it won't come anyway." We laughed again about "old Agnes" and their dog Booger, the yacht Lyle Dean, the Gendelman amateur hour, Wally, Carl Greyson, and anything else that came to mind from all the times we had listened together or separately and laughed about later.

My parents left again for points south a couple of days later but they both asked me to save things on my "confuser" (that one is for you Uncle Bobby) about his career on WGN. I printed out a couple of pictures and drawings to show them when they returned home.

I really think that in my younger days, the bond between my father and I, although not created by Uncle Bobby, was held in place long enough for us to understand that we are a lot alike. Remarkably, I have noticed that Bobby also is a part of my kids' lives, and they were also left saddened by his passing.

For a common guy, "y'all" screwed up the sense of humor for three generations of my family, and all I can say is thank you.

One Family's Letters from Bob

Harriet Ellis

Harriet Ellis lives in Chicago. She is a communication specialist and marketing expert.

Here are selected letters from Bob Collins to my brother, Richard Wilson, who had a correspondence with Bob over several years. My brother was a sports and entertainment photographer. He died of leukemia in July 1995.

Bob's attention made every difference in my brother's life. He waited to get these letters, and they always perked him up.

We will always appreciate what Bob Collins did for Dick. It shows the true measure of the man knowing how busy he must have been, but he still took time to write letters.

Just a quick note to thank you for all your letters. Sorry to keep reading that you're not doing so good. At least you can still walk around, like to the park and McDonald's. I think that's great.

Thanks for your kind words about waiting for me to come on the air every morning. I'm glad I can help in some way.

—Bob Collins, April 28, 1995

Sorry to read you don't like the Cub announcers. I happen to think they're great. You sure know a lot about baseball. I bet it was your dream to be a baseball player.

Take care and keep writing.

—Bob Collins, May 4, 1995

So now you've been in the hospital 22 times. I'm really sorry to hear that. It's nice to know that when you are in the hospital that they take such good care of you.

You sure met a lot of famous people in your lifetime. When you do, it's really nice to know that they usually turn out to be just regular people.

—Bob Collins, May 23, 1995

Richard, get the hell out of that hospital! Get better soon.

—Bob Collins, July 20, 1995

He was a Regular Guy, Homespun

Joseph Violante

Joseph Violante lives in Chicago and works in the restaurant business.

I can't remember when or exactly how I first started to listen to Bob on WGN, but I believe it was sometime in 1980 or 1981. I moved to the Chicago area in 1979, and my initial job here had me working nights. At the time Bob was working afternoon drive time, and Wally was doing morning drive.

In 1980 I began working days and spent a good part of the day in an office. I listened to WGN for the Cubs games to help pass the time in the afternoon.

On occasion I would leave the radio on when the game ended and listen to Bob. At the time I certainly was not a typical talk-radio fan; I was in my early 30s, but I was immediately attracted to Bob's show. Bob was just one of the guys; his down-to-earth style made me feel at home with him. Although I never met him, Bob became a friend.

When Bob switched to mornings, so did I. There were periods of time during the 16 years that I was friends with Bob that I couldn't listen to his show on a regular basis, but whenever I could I sought him out.

Times and jobs changed and after a couple of years of not being able to catch his show I became an early riser. Now I caught Bob starting at 5 each morning, and he kept me company each morning on my tedious drive to work.

I liked listening to Bob because he was Bob. Homespun, gregarious, to the point, and friendly. His show was always interesting and always entertaining. He treated everyone the same whether they were important dignitaries or just regular people calling in. He was direct yet polite, opinionated yet willing to listen. He loved life and lived it to the fullest.

Bob's show was an integral part of my day. He got me going each morning and prepared me for the day. I didn't always agree with what Bob said or with what he believed, but I always respected his opinion and his advice. It's strange how someone I never met became such a good friend.

I only saw Bob once in person. He was at the WGN radio booth at Taste of Chicago, and he projected the same personality live as he did on the air.

Like so many thousands of his listeners, I never talked to or met Bob, but all of us were certainly his friends.

I was fortunate enough to be listening to Bob the day of his last broadcast. That morning he read something written by someone else, which he stumbled upon and liked. It was called "Things I have learned since I aged."

It's fitting it was his last reading; it so personified Bob.

I was also listening to WGN that afternoon when the plane crash occurred.

I was driving out to New Lenox, Illinois, to see one of my daughters play basketball. Like the day of the Kennedy assassination, the events of that afternoon will stay vividly with me forever. When Spike O'Dell announced that the numbers on the plane's tail matched those of Uncle Bobby's plane, I was devastated.

I had lost one of my best friends. Mornings are not the same anymore. I really miss Bob.

The Only Man in a Group of Ladies

Anna Mae Goecking

Anna Mae Goecking lives in Chicago and is a retired homemaker.

I'm a real radio person. The first thing in the morning, I go into the kitchen, turn on the radio. For years it was Wally Phillips, and before him we listened to Eddie Hubbard. Now *that's* going way back.

Bob Collins came in on the afternoon. Not prime radio time. Then he moved up.

When he came on in the morning, boy, he was our man. What I liked about him is that he could be a rough, brusque character one day, then be soft as a big mushy teddy bear.

When I first heard Bob, I wasn't sure if I liked him. I think that was the same for a lot of us. We get a mindset for someone we like and we don't like big changes. He was a different type; much more rock 'n' roll. I guess he got that way when he worked in Milwaukee and California.

I had five kids and rock 'n' roll was not my style. We all learned to love Bob, though, and the way he was very touched by big stories.

The Baby Richard story was a big one for him. He had Bob Greene on a lot from the *Chicago Tribune*. Bob Collins never had kids of his own, but he was so touched by that family and what family meant to people. He kept a running commentary on the whole story.

He talked about the Baby Richard mom not telling the dad she was pregnant, the kid going off to foster parents, and how much they loved him, and then the dad finding out about the boy and wanting him back.

Bob Collins was on the side of the child. We thought the child belonged to the biological parents, but then there was this foster family that loved him.

Bob seemed to be as torn as the rest of us.

I will always remember when he called his mother and said, "Tell Daddy I love him." You couldn't imagine this big, tough guy being so gentle.

He never called his wife by her name, initially. She was just Old Agnes, and then eventually she was Christine. We got to know about their life together.

His younger sister was in California when there was an earthquake. He was worried about her and talked about it on the radio. We were worried about her, too, even though we didn't even know her.

You really felt like it was your family. You knew all about them, even though you wouldn't recognize any of them on the street.

He was a person who loved gadgets, any goofy gadget that was out there. Yet he was computer dysfunctional and sometimes telephone dysfunctional. I could identify with him on that!

I also liked when he talked about his dogs. I remember his one dog, Lady Rockwell, and then he ended up with Booger, who seemed to be a massive, drooling dog.

It's funny, when you try to remember things about Bob; it's hard because he was with us every day. It's like trying to tell a story from your own childhood, and sometimes you can't remember it.

We had a discussion the other day about the Kathy and Judy show on WGN. We just call them Kathy and Judy, like they live next door.

Bob was always in the kitchen in the morning. Even now, it's like I'm waiting for him to come back from vacation. I heard him talk that morning at 10 minutes to 9 about how he was leaving to go flying. Then around 4 that afternoon I heard that he might be dead. All of us old ladies took it quite to heart. We all called each other.

It seemed like a good friend was gone. It was such an everyday thing. You could be doing your own thing and not paying complete attention to him, and yet he was there. I'd get to the Riviera Country Club in Orland Park, Illinois, for water aerobics, and you'd automatically say, "Did you have your radio on in the car?" And someone who say, "Yeah! Did you hear Bob Collins?"

I spend much of my time with my women friends, and Bob filled a void for us. Bob was a male presence for us, like having a good friend around. If something was in the news, he brought it to our attention. It was like he was part of our group.

Cruising Alaska with Bob and Chris

Dolores Dalbec

Dolores Dalbec lives in Des Plaines, Illinois, and is a retired executive secretary.

Early in 1996, Bob announced on his morning show that he, along with Triple A, was planning an Alaskan cruise. If anyone was

Dolores Dalbec, Bob Collins, Christine Collins, Bill Dalbec

interested, they could call Triple A for more information. This sounded really good to us because my husband and I had always wanted to see Alaska. The "icing on the cake" was to be able to meet Bob and Christine and visit Alaska at the same time. We signed up for the cruise.

We received an invitation from our cruise hosts, Bob and Christine Collins, along with the Triple A tour directors. We were given the opportunity to meet our fellow Alaskan cruisers at a luncheon aboard the Odyssey on Lake Michigan. Most importantly, we got to meet Bob and Christine for the first time!

We traveled as a group from O'Hare to Vancouver, where we saw a bit of Vancouver while riding the bus from the airport to the ship, the Sun Princess. We saw Bob and Christine at the airports, but we were always a little hesitant to approach them, and mindful to respect their privacy.

Aboard ship, we were invited to several cocktail parties hosted by Bob, Christine, and Triple A. Of course, casual wear was suggested. I'm sure that was Bob's idea.

Each couple made its own itinerary. I do not recall seeing Bob and Christine on any of our adventures. They might have taken advantage of all that was offered but not at the same time or with our group.

The highlights of our Alaskan cruise were many. Flying from Juneau on a helicopter and landing on the Mendenhall Glacier. Cruising Glacier Bay with glaciers all around, a spectacular view. In addition to Juneau we visited Skagway and Sitka, all of them charming in their own special ways.

We have been longtime listeners of WGN. When Wally left, we honestly felt no one could ever replace him. Just goes to show you how wrong a person can be. Bob did so well, and when he went on vacation we couldn't wait until he returned. We started every morning with Bob and we were much better for it.

Bob covered all phases of daily living. He was so versatile, and there wasn't much he did not accomplish. Bob and Christine (Old Agnes) were really soul mates. I pray that we shall never forget him. He enriched our lives.

After Bob's plane accident, our lives can never be the same. We will go on, but it's not nearly as much fun as it used to be.

This Georgian Found Bob a Peach, But He Really Wanted Cracker Barrel

Charles Dalbec

Charles Dalbec is a career U.S. Army officer assigned to the U.S. Army Reserve Command in Fort McPherson, Georgia.

Besides being an avid listener to Bob on WGN radio, I had occasion to meet Bob while being stationed at Fort Sheridan. I began listening to WGN radio/television with Wally in the early 1960s. WGN was always a button on all of our radios, as well as Channel Nine on our televisions. Bob and I shared many conversations while I lived in Illinois and later when I moved to Conyers, Georgia. While I left Des Plaines for Atlanta in August 1991, my early-morning drives to Fort McPherson started off with Johnnie and Steve and then Bob.

In fact, Bob and I had exchanged many e-mail and telephone conversations when the Cubs came to play the Braves in the playoffs. While Bob looked for somewhere to stay, I told him I lived near the Cracker Barrel, and he was welcome to stay with the Dalbecs in Conyers.

Right about the time Bob would go on the air, I would be about 80 percent finished with my morning drive. You see, I live 35 miles east of Atlanta. Conyers is home of the Georgia International Horsepark, AT&T, and Heritage High School. I usually am able to listen to WGN until all of the other channels start up (usually about 6:30 a.m.). With the onset of the Internet, I can now listen to WGN Radio at all times, even though I live in Georgia.

My brother sent me a tape of Bob's audition, which Max Armstrong provided on the air. I listen to it whenever I need to smile, knowing that Bob is smiling with me.

The Carl Greyson Songbook Drive

Tom Holler

Tom Holler lives in Des Plaines, Illinois with his wife, Virginia.

My most vivid memory of Bob Collins occurred in the early 1980s. In those days Bob was on the afternoon-drive shift. Jim Loughman was the news/straight man, and Carl Greyson was still around somewhere.

The afternoon I'm thinking of was the origination of the Carl Greyson Memorial Songbook and Album. My wife (not an outdoors person) and I had attempted to head for Canada for a camping trip. We made it as far as Muskegon, Michigan, spent the night there, and my wife decided it was too cold, so we headed south toward Kentucky.

As we were driving south through Indiana, Bob was looking for suggestions for the songbook/album. People were calling in suggesting stuff by John Gary, John Davidson—dentist office/Wally Phillips-type music.

I almost had to pull off the road; we were laughing so hard.

It's hard to remember details almost 20 years later, but we both remember the afternoon and where we were, laughin' and scratchin' with Uncle Bobby.

In our opinion, a whole lot funnier than the Furtive Family of Fine Frogs.

Bob Didn't Try to Be Wally

Shirley Sheridan

Shirley Sheridan lives in Palatine, Illinois. She retired from sales and is now a computer operator.

I listened to Bob Collins when he started at the very beginning in the afternoon show. I followed him all the years, even when he filled in for Wally in the morning because I was listening to Wally.

I don't think there's a day I didn't listen to Bob. I used to get angry with him. I used to get happy with him. I used to disagree with him and I'd shut him off!

Nobody will ever be Bob Collins.

Another thing I liked about Bob is that he never tried to be Wally, and he said that. Bob and Wally were like night and day, and yet I liked both of them.

The thing I liked about Wally was his calm voice. You get up and you don't want to get bombarded with a lot. He had a calming effect.

He gave you the news in a nice, calm voice. He seemed always to be helping someone.

Bob was always up. You seldom heard him in the morning down. He'd come on and laugh about something that really wasn't even funny, and the next thing you knew you were laughing, too.

His crazy music, I loved it. I wouldn't sit down in my own home and play it, but in the morning to perk me up, I loved it.

I think he also really cared about people and wanted to help them. When someone called, he'd say, "I can't help you," on the air, but he said to leave the number and he'd help. I think he really did.

A lot of people hated him: "I wouldn't listen to that blowhard." But we're all like Bob in that respect. We have opinions that other people disagree with, and other people have opinions we don't like. But you kind of go along and don't make waves. Bob didn't care. This was his opinion, and you could take it or leave it. He used to say, "Hey, I'm not right in everything, but this is the way I feel about it."

It's a great loss. There are a lot of things he would have done, and we'll never know what he would have accomplished.

I listened to Bob so much; it was like having a member of the family in your kitchen. I remember when Bob went through his second divorce; he was a bitter person back then. He didn't like himself very much, and he didn't like the world very much. He thought he got a raw deal and he let everybody know about it.

Then it was forgotten. Then, when he married Christine, he became a different person. He really cared about her and he let everybody know it.

I think he was very young when he had the first divorce. The second divorce I think was mutual, but he felt bad about it.

It's like I've lost that member of my family. When you listen to somebody's voice every day, you care about them. The world has lost somebody who wasn't afraid to speak up for what he thought was right or wrong. I'll miss that.

I lost a cousin of mine in February, around the same time Bob died. I felt extremely heartbroken about my cousin, Donna. Yet I felt almost worse losing Bob because I listened to him every day and I spoke to Donna only a few times a year.

When you live alone, you're the only one here. When you get up in the morning, there's your companion until you get ready to leave.

I heard him the morning he died. He was talking about road rage and how people get so angry behind the car, and yet he was never afraid in the air. So it's ironic he died in the air, but not surprising because he wasn't afraid to fly. He loved it so much.

I'm not afraid to fly. I have a brother-in-law, Bob Bresson, who lives in Compton, Illinois. He has the Bresson Airport in Compton, southwest of Rockford. He's had that airport since he was a young boy. His grandfather taught him how to fly. I fly with Bob anytime I got out there. I love being in the plane. We fly over the cornfields and the farms. It's really beautiful up in the air. Very peaceful. I can understand why Bob Collins loved it so much.

Sometimes things happen to us when we're doing things we really care about, and we'll never know why.

My Mom Was Addicted to Bob

Corinne Belisle Madden

Corinne Belisle Madden lives in Chicago. She and her husband, Dave, have three children, Shannon, Sean, and Killian. She is pursuing a master's degree in education. Corinne is a founding member of Crop Shop, a photo-album club. One of the highlights of cropping, aside from the beautiful memory albums, is the opportunity to trim off strangers, to make yourself look skinnier à la photo liposuction, and to cut away people you do know but don't like.

Looking at the calendar, there must have been life before Bob, but I don't remember it. My dad had been dead a few years when Mom started saying, "Bob this and Bob that." Then she did it: She referred to him as "Uncle" Bobby. I wasn't that naive; some of my friends had uncles who weren't uncles, so I figured she was getting ready to tell me she had met someone special.

Mom certainly did encounter a special man. We both did. For a man who had no children, he succeeded in raising a generation and then some. I grew up with Bob. Like any teen/adult interaction, we had a love/hate relationship. I often disagreed, but he never seemed to notice. Uncle Bobby just made sure you heard and understood his point, and that is a bit of an understatement.

In the beginning, Bob joined us for the ride home and early dinners.

Later, he woke us for work and school, and talked and laughed that wonderful laugh, all through breakfast and the morning drive. I went away to college, moved out, and married. Mom wasn't really alone. For years, Bob filled several voids in Mom's life. Some things as simple as a man's booming voice and infectious laugh reverberating through the house were a complex companionship with no strings attached.

When I heard Bob had died, I felt great sadness and guilt. It had been a while since I, independent of my mother's presence in my home or car, had tuned in, and I felt regret at having missed the opportunity of recently hearing him. It's the kind of Irish guilt you feel when you really meant to call or stop to visit someone, and you get the call that it is too late, your friend/relative is dead. In addition to being stunned at such an incredulous news report, I knew that my mom would be heartsick. Mom was addicted to Bob.

He was like a morning coffee to a caffeine addict or a cigarette to a chain smoker escaping from a no-smoking zone.

I wonder if Bob realized what he meant to so many people? Bob was hired as the talk-show host who was needed to fill a radio station's time slot.

Little did the first listeners realize that Bob was to become an honorary member of their immediate families. To the man behind the voice who filled an otherwise silent room with lively conversation, I thank you. To the man behind the voice who provided audio companionship, I thank you. To the man behind the voice who reminded a young widow that it's okay to laugh, I thank you, Uncle Bobby, and my father would have thanked you.

Lt. Col. John Cheyne, Marjorie Cheyne and Bob Collins

Tears for JFK and Bob Collins

Virginia Belisle

Virginia Belisle lives in Merrionette Park, Illinois. "Gin" to her family and friends, she loves life and wants to live forever. Since retiring as an adult probation officer, she spends her time reading, photo-cropping, and listening to classical, romantic, and Irish music. She enjoys playing cards and meeting her dearest friends for breakfast. She says her biggest hobby is spending time with her three grandchildren. Gin is an associate in the Community of the Sisters of Little Company of Mary. She's faithful to the Chicago police, family, friends, and her cats, Cubbie and Bear.

When asked to relate my feelings about the death of our friend, Bob Collins, my first thought was a quote that pretty much sums up my feelings and those of many of my dearest friends: "Some people come into our lives and leave footprints on our hearts, and we are never, ever, the same."

My radio is unaware of the fact that there is any other station besides WGN. Starting with Bob right on through the day ending with Johnnie and Steve. I wish I had a dollar for every time Bob Collins was quoted by me since his arrival in Chicago on the late-afternoon show and eventually the morning show.

It was funny. Every time I was in someone else's car on the way to work, the driver would automatically turn the knob to Bob for me. I can't tell you how many people I turned on to Uncle Bobby. When you would tune in for Bob and immediately remember he was on vacation, it was a letdown. But when he was there, it was great! So many of his expressions will always be remembered. Favorites include Bob's comments after an argumentative caller disconnected: "He's nothing but a bed-wetting commie!" And his jovial-voiced "my fine, big body."

For more than 15 years my only sister, Corinne Madden, lived in Michigan. She shares the name with my daughter. And she, too, is a Collins fan. When we talked on the phone or had our visits, it was always, "How did you like what Bob said?" I always knew she was tuned in to Bob, and it just felt so good to have something so personal to share over the miles and through the years.

I received several expressions of condolences after Bob's death. Former co-worker, carpooler, and dear friend Cathy Spencer Moran, knowing how devastated I would be, called to extend sympathies when she heard about the crash. Cathy, although not a morning person herself, was one I had turned on to Bob.

Mary Dewan, another of my dear friends, and I had previously arranged to go somewhere on the day that turned out to be the day of the funeral. However, neither of us even considered leaving the house while the funeral mass was being televised.

That reminds me how very often Bob quoted his Baltimore Catechism: "You don't have to understand it—it's a mystery." Well, its no longer a mystery to Bob, is it? Didn't he love the City of Chicago, the Marine Corps, the Chicago Police and the Fire departments, the Salvation Army, animals (mostly Booger), and kids, but most of all, his Old Agnes.

In all of my 71 years, I have only cried at the passing of two celebrities, both young and both tragically killed: John Kennedy and Robert L. (as in "lovable") Collins. I miss Bob. I miss his laugh, I miss his humor and how he wasn't afraid to show his emotions, but most of all, because I lost a really good friend.

Bye Uncle Bobby.

Searching for Bob's Harley

Jeanne Fischer

Jeanne Fischer lives in Clinton, Wisconsin. She owns a travel agency in Clinton, where they listen to WGN every day.

I grew up near Lake Geneva. So I like to go there and visit. I used to look for Bob all the time around there. When I listened to him in the morning, he would talk about taking his Harley and going up to Lake Geneva. I'd tell my husband, "Let's see if we can find Bob!"

I thought that maybe I'd get to meet him and he'd talk about it the next day on the radio. So, we'd go over there on a Sunday afternoon, and I'd always look for him. Whenever I'd see a group of Harley motorcycles, I'd see if he was one of them.

He was pretty recognizable, so if he were there, I would have seen him. You know all the times I looked, I never spotted him! Not once.

After Bob died, I told my husband, "Oh darn, I'm not going to be able to look for him, anymore." It was a little game I played with Bob, and he didn't even know it.

I felt like I knew him. I had so much fun always looking for him because, in a way, it was my opportunity to bond with him. I was excited by the possibility of actually spotting him, let alone getting a chance to talk with him or say something to him.

I would have told him how much I enjoyed listening to him. We woke up to him every morning. He was our alarm clock. I was listening to him as long as he was on the station. I've lived in this area all my life, and I've listened to WGN since I was in college in the late '60s.

I liked his sense of humor. I can't even tell you a joke he said or an example of something I found funny. I thought all of it was funny. He made me laugh every day.

The radio is tuned to WGN at my travel agency. We listened to it every day. I know two other women in the office are big WGN fans, too. It gave us something to talk about.

Bob cared about people, and I liked that, too. You could just tell he cared about people, the way he reacted to his listeners. I remember the day they had the earthquake out in California and Bob talked with his sister. She was naturally upset. He was all concerned and caring for her.

I go to the YMCA in Beloit in the morning for an exercise class. Whenever I get to class, one of the first things we talk about is Bob Collins and what he said that day on the radio. He has a lot of fans in this area.

I've always talked about him as Uncle Bobby. He's like your uncle or your next-door neighbor. He was a real person, not somebody you just heard on the radio.

When he was killed, it was very emotional. It was like losing a close friend. I couldn't get the funeral on the television up here, but I listened to it on the radio.

It was the topic of conversation no matter where you went for days.

Garry, Roe, Mayor Daley, and Bob

Carol Bibat

Carol Bibat lives in Chicago and is a secretary.

My husband, Ben, and I started listening to Bob when he had the afternoon show. It was in the car on the way home from work. He was so different from what they had on WGN in the morning.

I think that by nature afternoon shows are more abrasive and abrupt with people. I think in the morning you want calm and quiet, but on the way home it's fun to hear something livelier. That's what

Bob Collins was. He was abrupt with his listeners. He was some-times rude to them. But I enjoyed him.

Depending on my mood, I sometimes find that entertaining and funny to listen to people say, "Oh, my gosh, how can you talk that way!"

Then he got on the morning show and Uncle Bobby appeared. It was a whole different personality. He became more personable. He talked like he was everybody's friend. That's why it was so shock-ing when he died. His voice was so familiar; his laugh was so famil-iar. You knew he liked motorcycles, airplanes; it was like he was a friend, not a famous person removed from you. More like your next-door neighbor.

On the day he died, I was listening to Garry and Roe on WLS. They started talking about this airplane crash. They were saying, "Why are they making a big deal out of this. It happens all the time." Later, they were saying, "Oh, the plane crashed into a hospital and that's why everybody's reporting it."

It was true, no matter what station you turned on, they were talking about this plane crash.

Then it came out that it was Bob Collins. And Garry and Roe, two of the most irreverent people who make fun of everything, became respectful of the whole situation.

It was interesting to hear that played out in a long sequence of information.

The other day I was thinking about Bob Collins and how he came across as a regular guy. Because I think Mayor Daley is that same way. They come across as regular guys. The mayor gets flus-tered and defensive. But that's real life. We all get that way.

When the mayor's son has a party in their summer home and gets in trouble, we all feel for him because we know what he's going through. The mayor doesn't take care of his health and ends up in the hospital. We can all relate to that.

If you look at why Mayor Daley and Bob Collins are so suc-cessful, it's because they're regular people who relate to regular people. Just like the guy next door.

Memories of a Tailgate Party with Bob

Steven R. Campbell

Steven R. Campbell lives in Laurinburg, North Carolina, where he is minister of the Laurinburg Christian Church.

Early August in Chicago marks the first of the pre-season NFL games for the Bears. In 1985 the Bears were going to host the Tampa Bay Buccaneers. WGN's new contract as the radio home for the Bears meant a big tailgate party before the game.

My fiancée, Terrie, and I headed north on Lake Shore Drive toward Soldier Field. As we pulled even with the back of the WGN stage, there he was, leaning on the chain-link fence: Bob Collins. Instinctively I waved as though he was an old friend. Bob leaned back from the fence, smiled his patented smile, and waved back. Forty-five minutes later we were eating hot dogs and watching Bob and Chuck Swirsky banter for 10 minutes. I shook his hand and he took notice of the "big orange cap" I was wearing. As genuine as his radio persona, Bob was as friendly, open, and approachable as the guy next door.

Radio should be fun, informative, and fasted-paced. Bob (one "o") Collins (two "l"s) was a master. My appreciation for Bob happened by accident. I was preaching in a small church in Polo, Illinois, while attending seminary in Lincoln, Illinois. Such an arrangement required a long drive through the heartland of Illinois on Monday and Wednesday afternoons. After a baseball game, I left the radio tuned to WGN. This crazy entertaining guy kept me listening. I was hooked. Who else could get away with playing Frank Sinatra back to back with David Allen Coe? Bob introduced me to the music of Steve Goodman. For that I am thankful.

One afternoon, Bob had a guest on to talk about shyness. Before long I found myself on the telephone describing how a guy who can stand in front of a congregation every week gets sweaty palms when he has to talk to people one-on-one. The conversation was more like something that happens across the kitchen table. I never considered myself someone who would call a radio talk show. Bob put me at ease and learned something besides. Now that's great radio! That's why I listened.

My favorite times were when Bob would declare that he was going to "play" on the radio. There would be no deep discussions or controversial guests. We would hear rock 'n' roll trivia. Maybe there would be a replay of Furtive Family of Fine Frogs. One day, while playing on the radio, Bob decided he could write a cheap, trashy novel. Every day he'd add a scene with the collaboration of a listener. I got the privilege of opening chapter two.

Four to six weeks later, I received a package from WGN radio. Within a square box was a gift certificate for True Value Hardware, a cushy padded toilet seat, and my pride and joy, a "big orange cap." I pull it off the shelf from time to time and wear it around the house. It's a reminder of why I listened to Bob Collins.

She Thought Bob Sounded like Santa Claus

Jane Parman

Jane Parman lives in Chicago. A single mother of two teenagers, she works part-time as a school librarian.

I used to listen to Wally Phillips and was a fan of WGN, so it was natural for me to listen to Bob Collins. I liked the soothing sound of his voice. To me it was comforting and soothing. It was trustworthy.

I had the radio on in the car the day I heard about the plane crash, never thinking by any chance that it was Bob. I didn't know it was a hobby of his. I later saw it on the TV news and was shocked. I'm still in shock. I remember thinking, "What a loss," but when I listened to what he did in his life outside of the radio, he was quite a daredevil, and I didn't know that part of him.

He wanted to live life to the fullest; he didn't want to miss anything.

When I would go to work or school in the morning, I would turn Bob on first thing. The first two things I'd do: start the car and turn on the radio. I knew he'd be there as I was driving, almost like he was a passenger in the car. I always listened to whatever topic he was talking about.

People being opinionated doesn't bother me. I don't take sides myself. I'm not a very politically interested person, but I'm more interested in the subject at hand. I like to know what all the sides of an issue are. Bob's show was really nonpolitical. I know people say he was politically connected or had friends in politics, but it wasn't really reflected on his show. If he felt strongly about an issue, he felt strongly about it. And it didn't matter whom it was, whether it was the governor or the mayor of Chicago. I thought Bob was actually nonpolitical.

I liked that he treated the politicians with respect for the offices they held. He'd say, "Mayor, thank you for stopping." Like he was walking by and Bob just invited him in; "Come on, let's talk." They must have appreciated that because they were so willing to come on and talk. It made for interesting debates.

I really miss Bob. For some people, he was a father figure, a part of your family. The sound of his voice was

Roy Stanek

comforting; he was funny. He sounded like Santa Claus, this comforting older person.

Since his death, I've let my daughter take over the radio. I
haven't turned WGN back on; I haven't listened to any other radio
talk show. I just don't want to turn it on because the first few times
I turned on WGN, it sounded creepy without Bob. His voice wasn't
there.

He made you want to listen, period! I can still hear his voice.

I never call in to radio shows. But one day, Rich Daley was
supposed to be on his show and the mayor was late. Bob asked on
the air of anyone listening ever did scheduling for a politician, so I
called in! I used to work for Gov. Dan Walker scheduling his ap-
pointments in Springfield. So I knew something about the topic.
Bob said he hadn't lived in Illinois long, and he didn't know the
name "Dan Walker." We talked for a while until Rich Daley arrived.

I worked with the mayor years ago when we had the Illinois
Constitutional Convention in 1970. Rich Daley was a delegate to
the convention. I worked on that convention. But I hadn't talked
with him until that day he was on Bob Collins.

I asked Mayor Daley if he remembered me, and he said, "Janie,
how are you?" That meant a lot to me. I was able to connect with
an old friend through Bob. How often can you say that?

Pickin' Up Bob Cross-Country

Charlie Wall

*Charlie Wall is a 48-year-old truck driver from Central Pennsylvania, mar-
ried with a 12-year-old daughter. He's been driving professionally for almost 25 years, is active in his local volunteer fire department, and sings in
his church choir.*

If you look in the Clearfield, Pennsylvania, Bell Atlantic phone
book, you will find 44 names listed under Collins. You will even
find two Robert Collins listed. If you ask anyone in or around the

Clearfield/Curwensville area if they know Bob Collins, more than likely they'll ask you, "the one that lives out in East End, or the one that lives in Glen Richey?"

Humbling? Perhaps. Ego-deflating? Maybe. I can't truthfully say that I knew the Bob Collins who was the legend at WGN that well. What I can say is that the guy I grew to love hearing on the radio first thing in the morning when I was in Chicago was truly unique. I've been driving over the road for almost 25 years, and I have my favorite radio stations in every area of the country that I see. I listen to radio according to my moods; most times I listen to country music. Sometimes I listen to oldies. Still other times I might listen to jazz, classical, or Top 40. So what kept me coming back to WGN and Bob Collins?

When I first started to drive commercially, all I wanted to hear on my radio was rock 'n' roll. But as I grew older and some-what wiser, my needs changed. I can't really say when I first tuned in to Uncle Bobby, but the first time I did, something about him just sort of reached out and said, "I've got you, and you will not want to let go." The voice was nothing really out of the ordinary, but the laugh and the sense of humor were what hooked me.

While I obviously couldn't listen every day of the week, when I was able to tune in, I never heard Bob be rude or short with anyone, although God knows there were times when he should have been.

I actually got to talk to Uncle Bobby one day. It was during the presidential campaign in 1992, and he was relating a story of a woman in Mississippi who had been victimized by an intruder. With-out going into specifics, she related to the court that "I got 'em," and that's what prompted me to call in. My exact words to Bob when he answered the phone were, "If I can borrow a line from the Democrats, I feel his pain." That's when I heard that trademark laugh, and that's what I miss right now. That infectious laugh. It didn't matter how long I had been sitting in traffic surrounded by the largest group of horses' asses to ever get behind steering wheels, when I heard that laugh, the anger just sort of disappeared. Bob Collins had a way of making your troubles a little easier to bear.

I've heard so many stories about him that he almost seemed like he was bigger than life. I never did get to meet him in person, and I had no idea what he even looked like until about a year or so ago when I visited WGN's website. When I first saw Bob's picture, I thought, "This is Bob Collins? He sure doesn't look like he sounds!" But looks can indeed be deceiving. That smile on his face made him look like anybody's next-door neighbor, someone you might go bowling with, or maybe kick back somewhere and have a couple beers with. Heck, I might even have asked to borrow his lawn mower if I wouldn't have had to go so far to return it.

When you grow up in a small town in central Pennsylvania that has a population of barely 500 people, you have neither the opportunity nor the pleasure of being exposed to someone like Bob Collins. I can remember the "Breakfast Club" with Don McNeil when I was in grade school, but I didn't even know where the program originated. The AM station that was closest to home was only 1000 watts strong and went off the air at sundown. I guess you could say I led a sheltered life when it came to radio personalities.

I'm not trying to canonize Bob Collins, although it may sound like I am. It's just hard to put into words what an impact he had on me when I never met him. (But I've tried to express my feelings in a poem I wrote called "Why?") You just knew when you heard "Good morning, y'all," the day was just going to be a little easier to face. Thanks for the smiles, Bob. I guess God needed a morning man more than we did. May your fine, furtive frogs live on as long as your legend.

Why?

The news came across my radio and I asked myself, Why?
Why did my radio just lie to me?
This didn't really happen; he's not really gone;
God doesn't punish like that; it's just too cruel.

He was everyone's uncle, related or not;
And more's the pity I didn't know him better.
I didn't live within the sound of his voice, and I'm the poorer for it;
Because I knew when I heard"Good morning, y'all"that the day was looking
    better.

Some day we'll all know why this had to happen;
When we meet again in heaven, it will all be made clear.
But for now, I console myself with this thought;
God needed a morning man.

Good bye, Uncle Bob; we love you.

Foot Stomping, Ass Kicking, Rock 'n' Roll

Mike Osenga

Mike Osenga lives in Brookfield, Wisconsin. He is a journalist and senior vice president of Diesel & Gas Turbine Publications.

Rock-'n'-roll AM radio in Milwaukee in the 1970s was a pretty tightly wrapped package. Talk; 2:32 song; commercial; 2:31 song; talk. Lotta music, not much talk. Hour after hour. We knew the voices were real; we'd seen the disc jockeys at sock hops once in a while. But they were mostly old white guys who usually looked nothing like they sounded. And besides, the music was the thing.

There were some personalities starting to emerge in FM radio, and certainly some big names in big cities. But in Milwaukee in 1971, they were mostly just voices, except for Bob Barry, "Beatle Bob." And this newcomer, *Collins, Bob Collins.*

To some of us Bob Barry represented "old" rock 'n' roll (as recently as three years ago!). Collins represented the new, hard-driving, foot-stomping, ass-kicking, rock 'n' roll!

I forget if Bob was working for WRIT or WOKY, the two big Milwaukee AM rock and roll stations (he worked at both), but wherever he was, he came on the air at 3 p.m., just about the time some of us were getting out of high school, legally or otherwise.

We'd hop in our cars and turn on the radio because Collins always, always started with something hot, usually Bob Seger or the Stones. We'd crank up the volume of those very bad radios and pound the steering wheel singing "Ramblin' Gamblin' Man" or "Katmandu" as we drove home. Rock 'n' roll!

One day we got in the cars, opened our windows, turned up the radios and heard—"Darling Be Home Soon" by the Lovin' Spoonful? "Darling Be Home Soon"?

A neat ballad, yeah sure. But Collins? "Darling Be Home Soon"? At 3?

I remember we sat quietly staring at the radio. "Darling Be Home Soon"?

I don't know if Bob was having marital troubles, or was just sad over a lady, but when the song ended he came on the air, in a raspy sad voice we hadn't heard before, and said, quoting from the song, "A quarter of my life has almost passed, and the time that I have wasted is the time I spent without you."

There was a pause that seemed to last forever. And then he played "Darling Be Home Soon," again.

We went nuts. The same song twice in a row! On AM! Outta site! Cooooool!!!!!

But at the same time, I also realized, maybe for the first time, that there was a person behind the voice. A real live person, who while we were in the parking lot at Muskego High School, was sitting behind a microphone somewhere. And he was hurting, and it sounded like he was hurting badly.

I don't know if I made the connection then, or ever, but maybe, maybe because of that spring day in the parking lot, the first thing I did when I started college that fall was sign up to work at the school's AM radio station.

Milwaukee joins Chicago in its grief over the loss of this very special man.

Roy Stanek

Thank you

Uncle Bobby